HAUNTED
HARTLEPOOL &
EAST DURHAM

HAUNTED
HARTLEPOOL &
EAST DURHAM

Paul Screeton

For Margaret O'Rourke –
a fellow seeker

First published 2014

The History Press
The Mill, Brimscombe Port
Stroud, Gloucestershire, GL5 2QG
www.thehistorypress.co.uk

British Library Cataloguing in Publication Data.
A catalogue record for this book is available from the British Library.

ISBN 978 0 7509 5235 4

Typesetting and origination by The History Press
Printed in Great Britain

CONTENTS

ABOUT THE AUTHOR

A 'Poolie' by birth, Paul Screeton came into this world at Grantully Nursing Home, perhaps fortuitously on a major geological fault line. Since then he has lived most of his life in Hartlepool and the major part of his journalistic career was spent in various roles at the *Hartlepool Mail*. His authorial debut was *Quicksilver Heritage*, the influential study of earth mysteries and ley-lines in 1974. His subsequent eleven published books have been diverse and include studies of railways in folklore, Hartlepool's monkey-hanging legend, two on dragonlore, contemporary legends (urban myths), local odd tales, a history of ley hunting, an appreciation of polymath John Michell, an anthology and most recently, *Quest for the Hexham Heads*, an in-depth work of investigative journalism into a Celtic mystery reverberating still in the twenty-first century. The supernatural elements in that study led Paul back to the paranormal in his own native North East England, where he and fellow journalist Margaret O'Rourke had been fascinated by local ghost report and collaborated on occasions. The result is a mature reflection on half a century's worth of collecting regional ghostlore and folk tales.

Paul is also an active folklorist, editing both magazine and Facebook forum under the name *Folklore Frontiers*. He has also created a website for sharing information on the North-East Coast Line and has been a rail enthusiast since 1956. He is chairman of Friends of Seaton Station. When he has time, he enjoys the siren call of tavernology.

INTRODUCTION

I was born in Hartlepool and will probably die here. But will I return to do a spot of haunting? I have no idea. However, it has been said that Hartlepool folk are very insular: they never leave the town and marry local people, yet whenever a major national or international disaster occurs, someone from Hartlepool will be there. Maybe it's because so many outsiders were attracted by jobs in industry and settled here, creating a diverse gene pool and the unique accent.

Geographically located in north-east England, Hartlepool is a town of 92,000 people and was previously part of County Durham, now to the north, where the former East Durham mining communities are a world apart in culture, outlook and dialect. But the supernatural knows no such arbitrary boundaries.

Administratively, East Durham is overseen by Durham County Council, while Hartlepool has become a unitary authority. However, until 1967, when the 'ancient borough' of Hartlepool and the larger West Hartlepool were amalgamated, both had been proud to have independent councils and go their separate ways. The 'shotgun marriage' saw a historic 'Old Side' – granted a charter by King John in 1201 – wed to a Victorian upstart created by economic rivalries during the Railway Mania. Headlanders, or Crofters as 'Old' Hartlepool folk were known, even had their own small fleet of four buses painted blue, whereas West Hartlepool's were red. Both had services to the Headland and many Crofters would shun the red and wait to 'pot' a blue.

The Railway Mania affected Old Hartlepool first, changing it from a sleepy fishing village into a bustling coal exporter. But a rival scheme making a pincer movement from the south created improved port facilities and gave birth to the fledgling West Hartlepool. Led by the pioneering activities of Ralph Ward Jackson, an increasing number of docks were created, the volume of coal for export increased and pit props for the mines imported. The area to the north also benefited from this enterprise, with many more collieries opening to take advantage of the rich seams of fossil fuel.

The original Hartlepool lies on a promontory overlooking the North Sea, while West Hartlepool grew westwards from Tees Bay. East Durham, by contrast, is higher and forms a plateau. This book covers Hartlepool as it is today, the villages Greatham, Elwick and Hart, to the north the post-war new town of Peterlee and the former pit villages, plus a hinterland delineated for demarcation purposes by another railway development, the current route of the East Coast Main Line.

The people of Hartlepool have only rare social contact with their East Durham cousins. However, when the young men of Blackhall, Horden and Peterlee converge on their more vibrant neighbouring town for weekend drinking and clubbing, the 'pit yackers' try to wind up 'Poolies' or 'Hartlepudlians' with jibes regarding the monkey-hanging legend, often leading to random disturbances. One example of graffiti is said to have read, 'Poolies are loonies, but Yackers are crackers'. A possible derivation is that yacker evolved from hacker (i.e. a coal hewer).

While the spectre of pit closures loomed like some almost visible, nearly tangible Grim Reaper over the villages of South-East Durham, the folklore associated with mining made virtually no mention of underground supernatural manifestations.

While Peterlee has attracted inward international investment, a more visible renaissance has boosted Hartlepool. The moribund dockland area has been transformed into a vibrant marina, with shopping, housing, eating and drinking establishments, plus tourist attractions at the Historic Quay. Satellite resort Seaton Carew has a splendid beach and the Headland boasts the magnificent abbey church of St Hilda.

Hartlepool has been the butt of many jokes, but lived to tell the tale. And what a tale! During the Napoleonic Wars a French ship was wrecked and the only survivor, washed ashore, was a bedraggled monkey dressed in a military uniform. Suspecting it to be spy, the fishermen held an al fresco court, found it guilty and hanged the gibbering simian in an act of ignorant yet cautionary zeal.

Indeed, legends aplenty are part of Hartlepool's fabric. It has been claimed that the prose poem *Beowulf* has its geographical setting at Hartlepool and Hart, the Scots King Robert the Bruce was born in Hart and the deeds of King Arthur are writ largely across East Durham. In fact, the doughty Arthur's mythos here is largely spectral and this book looks at many historical ghosts alongside more modern hauntings. Pubs figure widely, as might be expected from the region which gave the world Andy Capp, created by Hartlepool cartoonist Reg Smythe. Also, the local brewery is a veritable hive of paranormal activity. Other spectres share council and private houses, clubs, schools, roads, ships and a former airport.

I investigated several of these cases myself as a journalist with the *Hartlepool Mail* and many others are archived from that local paper's columns. Some I collected while researching and writing this book. I have also had experiences with the paranormal, which I share here. That said, I must admit to leaning towards being a sympathetic sceptic. As a seasoned journo, I know only too well the pitfalls of gullibility and have always been wary of anyone approaching a newspaper with a story – often as not they have a private agenda. But when the wheat has been sorted from the chaff, there are plenty of cases worthy of taking seriously and these are the ones which I am presenting on these pages.

As for explanations, I personally have no answers. I am a journalist and not a paranormalist, but I do feel qualified to comment as I have studied the subject for half a century. I do know the theories and will introduce these briefly where they have relevance.

So, be prepared for an entertaining and I hope erudite tour of a town rich in history and a region where (allegedly) King Arthur stamped his presence. As well as visiting many spooky locations, I even wrote the majority of this book in a haunted alcove of a pub – as I explain later – so join me for a glass or two. Draw the curtains, dim the lights, choose your favourite chair and immerse yourself in a journey into the realms of the unfathomable.

Paul Screeton, 2014

ONE

HISTORICAL HAUNTINGS (HARTLEPOOL)

SOME of the oldest buildings on Hartlepool's Headland have one thing in common: they all share regular visitations from a ghost, always referred to as the Grey Lady. She flits among the gravestones of the landmark which dominates the 'ancient borough', the magnificent abbey church of St Hilda. She patrolled the corridors of St Hilda's Hospital and could be found underground in the cellars of a nearby pub, undeterred by its bricked-up passages. She went back to school and terrified a hardened veteran soldier beneath the premises and has even been associated with Old Hartlepool's former municipal headquarters.

But who was – and is – she?

The identity of the Grey Lady is open to speculation, but my guess is that she is St Hilda herself. After leaving Hartlepool, she went on to find greater fame by founding Whitby Abbey. She had started as a humble nun named Hieu, whose vision was to create a monastery on the promontory at Hartlepool, and it was she who guided its fortunes from 649–657.

Her name is remembered in Hartlepool for what has been described as 'the finest of the parish churches of the North of England', and St Hilda's church is believed to stand upon the foundations of her Saxon monastery. Perhaps she hankered after her roots and her spirit returned to where her faith originally blossomed.

To confuse matters, the Headland also had a friarage and commentators over the decades have suggested that the Grey Lady may be male – to scant local support. Let's just say that I'm in favour of the more feminine argument, though as will be seen there has been some sturdy opposition.

The ghost glides through the churchyard that bears her name, passing the grave of the Victorian showman clown Billy Purvis, who played a role in another Hartlepool controversy – the hanging of a monkey during Napoleonic times. Perhaps her favourite haunt was St Hilda's Hospital, in Middlegate, until its closure in 1984. The hospital was built in 1865 with additions during the 1930s. However, the two-storey children's ward was originally a mid-sixteenth-century mansion with Elizabethan windows, shorn of their mullions. To conservationists' dismay the whole edifice was demolished in 1987. Numerous stories in the *Hartlepool Mail* have recorded the apparition being sighted in various parts of this sprawling hospital. I will quote one that is typical, from a letter by Doreen Lee, of Keswick Street, Hartlepool:

The Grey Lady was often seen floating around at night in her grey cloak. I was doing a spell of night duty on the orthopaedic ward. Having just completed a round of the patients at 2am, a young patient asked me for a drink of water. He then told me he had already asked me once, but remarked: 'You didn't reply, you just floated past my bed in your grey cloak.' The point is, I didn't have a grey cloak, mine was navy with a red lining. Also I was the only nurse on duty on that ward that night and I had been in the office for the past hour completing my daily report. So who had he seen 'floating past'? Could it have been the Grey Lady!

Hartlepool Mail reporter Margaret O'Rourke noted that St Hilda's Grey Lady might have been a woman dressed in an old-fashioned nursing uniform or perhaps a Grey Friar, for the foundations of a former Franciscan friarage's domestic

One theory regarding the Grey Lady's identity is that she was abbess at St Hilda's abbey church, seen here dominating the Headland. (Author's collection)

buildings (established around 1250, dissolved courtesy of Henry VIII) extended under the children's ward. To distinguish themselves, Franciscans wore grey, whereas Dominicans were the Black Friars and the Carmelites were White Friars. Local historian Walter Gill explained: 'They all wore long tunics (skirts down to their ankles), each order with its appropriate colour – and they were all men!'

If historical and archaeological evidence was on the side of demythologising, romanticism and folklore were not. Fellow journalist Bernice Saltzer introduced the human dimension:

> Legend has it that a Franciscan friar and a nun fell in love and planned their elopement during one of their secret meetings in the passageways beneath the Headland. The monks discovered the plan and murdered the brother and when the nun discovered his fate she committed suicide. She is also known as the Grey Lady and is believed to walk around the grounds of the former St Hilda's Hospital – where the tunnel leads – looking for her lost love.

Bernice's article was based on research by ghost hunter Garry Baker, who had spoken to a retired sister who worked at the hospital and wished to remain anonymous. In a rare example of vocal interaction, she claimed to have spoken to the Grey Lady and was told, 'You have a rest and I'll take over.' Another – not so helpful or friendly – aspect related to a nurse returning to a room she had recently tidied only to find the contents strewn about, despite the fact that no one could have been in it. As for the claims of a labyrinth of tunnels below the Headland, these include St Hilda's church being linked with various parts of the 'ancient borough', ranging from the cellars of the Seamen's Mission on the Town Wall, to The Globe and King's Head pubs. Certainly there are two bricked-up entrances in the cellars of the nearby Cosmopolitan pub; one leading in the direction of the friarage site and the other towards St Hilda's church. So, off to the pub ...

Located at the corner of Durham Street and Middlegate, according to one reference 'The Cos', as it is popularly known, was originally built for John Hart as an 'ale store'. Licensees in the mid-1980s, Don and Hazel Thynne cashed in on the tales of the ghost by running a Grey Lady carvery. She was also afforded another explanation for her presence and an identity as the former abbess of St Hilda's church, who would hide here with her companions when the Vikings were plundering, pillaging and raping. Giving the tale gloss, Bernice Saltzer romanticised that she fled carrying all the valuable religious artefacts through a secret tunnel from the church to a neighbouring fortress, reputedly on the site where The Cosmopolitan now stands. It is the cloaked abbess, protecting her possessions from the invading barbarians, who reputedly haunts the pub. Actually, despite local belief and media hyperbole, I can find no witness to a Grey Lady at the pub over the many decades, sponsored spook-ins and a visit by UK Living channel's *Most Haunted* team. It seems more likely that archaeological excavations on the Headland during 1972 and 1974 – plus renovation work to properties in the close vicinity – disturbed the psychic dimension.

The landlord during the early 1970s was John Foggerty. In July 1972 he fled from the cellars after experiencing a strong sense of fear and evil, and a feeling of being surrounded by something intangibly unpleasant. 'I was almost paralysed with fear. Whatever it was it was evil. I was cleaning out one of the lines, and when I managed to pull myself free from what seemed like being enclosed in a tight space, I ran upstairs leaving the water running. It was so bad I was frightened to go down alone,' he recalled. Another landlord, Mick Watson, had heard a tale that a nun was found in one of the tunnels by smugglers who thought she was spying on them, so they killed her. In his version it is she who walks the tunnels to the cellar.

The Grey Lady's perambulations extended in all directions beyond the hospital and at Henry Smith School she is connected with the cellars. Radio presenter, columnist and former teacher Alan Wright was a pupil at the school when there was one adult the pupils feared above all others: not a teacher or the headmaster, but the caretaker. But even this hard-as-nails war veteran who saw service in the trenches refused point blank to go back in the cellars after encountering the Grey Lady, who had approached and then passed through him. He recalled the hooded figure appearing to be very small and her legs stopping at her knees. The school had been built over the Franciscan friars' land and the original graveyard extended into where the cellar lay. According to revelations from an archaeological excavation, the ground level would have originally been 18 inches below the cellar floor – explaining the spook's lack of visible leg below the knee.

This is similar to the scare apprentice-plumber Harry Martindale had in 1953 while installing a new central heating system in the cellars of the Treasurer's

The Cosmopolitan, where the Grey Lady has made many appearances. (© Paul Screeton)

House in York. On this occasion the worker fell off his ladder in shock when a cart horse ridden by a Roman soldier and then several others, dressed in rough green tunics and plumed helmets, carrying short swords and spears, appeared through a brick wall – on their knees! All was explained when they reached a recently excavated area and it became clear that they were swalking on the old Roman road buried 15 inches below the surface!

Eventually the monks' quarters became Friarage Manor House and formed part of the original Hartlepool Hospital, later to be named St Hilda's Hospital, hence more sightings there. Because of the nature of the friarage, historians open-minded to ghostlore have concluded that the Grey Lady is not female but a wraith of a Franciscan male – a Grey Friar!

Male or female, the spectre has also been associated with the Victorian-era Borough Buildings, in Middlegate, built in 1866. This impressive edifice has had a long and chequered career, having variously accommodated a spacious entertainment hall area – 'home of the stars' it boasted – hosting variety shows, dancing, boxing and wrestling, plus a police station, library and tradesmen, such as a butcher's and a jeweller's. Apart from the Grey Lady, whose haunting is vague, another wraith that would

Henry Smith School, Hartlepool, was another building which attracted the Grey Lady's wanderings. (Author's collection)

appear briefly was an elderly man wearing an old-fashioned overcoat, seen during renovation of the bar. Speculation suggests that the police station was formerly here and so the sightings occurred on the site of the cells. It is further surmised that the ghost was a former boxer who got into a fight outside a hardware store and it took six policemen to restrain him and take the pugilist into custody.

It has also been claimed that the closed Croft Tower was a no-go area for many. In 1980 a plumber working in the ladies' toilet was spooked upon hearing a bell ring and seeing curtains move. Perhaps not your bog-standard spirit!

To briefly return to the Grey Friar notion, other commentators have speculated about phantom cowel-wearing monkish figures. Eerie 'hoodies' have trodden these shores since Gallic Celts introduced the cult of Genii Cucullati in Romano-British times. There is a shadowy reference to ghost hunter Garry Baker coming across sightings of ghostly monks at a house in Glastonbury Walk, on an estate in Throston, Hartlepool. A monastery was reputed to have been on the site many centuries ago. This seems too good to be true, for the road's name is so palpably evocative of a romantic mystical past. Seatonian Michael Dickinson told me he saw a group of half-a-dozen or so hooded figures in the 1970s, stood outside Holy Trinity church, Seaton Carew.

Cameron Hospital, in the former West Hartlepool's Serpentine Road, is where both my children were born. However, the hospital is no more, having been demolished after maternity facilities transferred to what is now the University Hospital of Hartlepool. Built with the generosity of the local Cameron brewing dynasty, the hospital

The Old Side Borough Buildings are still going strong and although associated with the Grey Lady, she has a gentleman rival or beau! (© Paul Screeton)

had supposedly been haunted from 1907 onwards, when a young nurse named Maud died from complications which set in after she was struck on the nose by a hysterical patient. The haunting was generally confined to the south, north and labour wards, and although not discussed publically for fear of ridicule, it was common knowledge within the staff community. A sense of unease associated with Maud's presence would unerringly presage a calamity. Cameron staff believed Maud was sad at the impending closure and demolition; one even claiming to have seen her spectre wringing her hands. There had been a plaque erected in her memory and when it was removed in preparation for the move, a large chunk of plaster fell into the anaesthetic department. Hours after the Cameron was vacated, security guard John Davison heard movement

in an upper corridor and eerie laughter, but a search assured him he was alone. He admitted to being 'terrified, absolutely terrified'.

As stated, Cameron Hospital owed its existence to a bequest from the local brewing company and despite so many brewery closures over the years, Hartlepool's Lion Brewery is still going strong. In fact, its fame rests largely on a beer called Strongarm. A contemporary legend claims that when a suitable name was being sought for a special new brew, either the chairman or head brewer looked out of the window at the warehouse of Foster & Armstrong and came up with the anagram Strongarm. Brewery Tap landlady and Camerons brewery guide, Marie-Louise McKay, gave me a special tour one Wednesday afternoon, including parts that the more general explanatory tour misses out, but are within bounds for plucky ghost hunters. I had no fears as Marie-Louise had told me beforehand that 'all the spirits are nice. There's never any malicious behaviour. I've never felt scared going through the brewery, even in the dark.' One very large long room, which is used only for archiving and the storage of valuables, was previously used for hop storage. Consequently, the loft was refrigerated and has massive thick doors which cannot be opened from the inside. Legend tells that a young worker was accidentally locked inside over a weekend and froze to death. Incarcerated where 'no one can hear you scream', his spirit has been blamed for moving furniture, hiding and then replacing items and placing boxes on to the floor off the shelves.

Similarly, in what is now a storeroom, the goods awaiting distribution had to be rearranged as they were blocking the path where the formidable matriarch Jane Waldon, of the founding brewery-owning dynasty, still walks, despite dying in 1860. Workers have heard her footsteps and the rustle of her skirt. The movement of objects in the way of her perambulation were noted on CCTV even when the door was locked and no human was caught on camera. Then, during a ghost-hunting party's visit, a blurred photograph was taken of a man in period costume, high up in the window of the head brewer's office. On other occasions, school groups were shown the original fermentation room, containing eight large vessels. More than one group – especially girls – would

A handy watering hole for generations of Hartlepool Mail journalists, yet none encountered the Grand Hotel's non-optics spirits. (© Paul Screeton)

Watch out for a spooky encounter in the corridors of Seaton Carew's Marine Hotel. (© Paul Screeton)

scream or shout out that an invisible presence had pulled their hair. 'A medium has told us that the supervising brewer is only drawing attention to the long hair and that it should be covered up. Girls were never employed by the brewery in the olden days,' related Marie-Louise. She also showed me the site of the well, lying next to buildings which were originally used as stables for the dray horses. Many visitors have reported their legs being kicked or the feeling that a large beast was pushing them out of the way.

Another Hartlepool landmark is one of the town's undoubted architectural masterpieces, the 1899-built opulent Grand Hotel, built of red brick with yellow terracotta in the style of a French château. When management decided to use the spacious haunted cellar to create a subterranean drinking area called the Coble Bar, the mischievous resident spirit turned its attentions to the public. Men reported being pushed by the over-familiar assailant while 'spending a penny', toilet doors refused to open or the doors would suddenly bang shut loudly and there would be the sound of flushing when no one was in any cubicle. On the floors above, chambermaids avoided one of the three former staff quarters up a private staircase, used latterly by trainee representatives of the previous railway-owning company. The room was said to be haunted by a girl who died in some unknown tragic circumstance.

More Victorian-era magnificence is afforded at Seaton Carew's Marine Hotel. An Art Nouveau creation, dating from 1900 and on the site of the former Seven Stars inn, its venerable age may account for a female wraith in period dress, seen several times in an upstairs passageway by night porter Keith Laidlaw. His granddaughter Cheryl Thompson is one of the bar staff reluctant to venture into the cellar. Members of staff have told me they feel it is creepy and Cheryl's granddad spoke of disconnecting pipes to clean the lines and fixing them back in place, but returning to find them again disconnected.

There's no need to linger long at what was formerly West Hartlepool Airport as all I have to go on is a single paragraph from an article. Previously known as Greatham Airport, it opened in April 1939 but was quickly commandeered as a pilot-training base and its airmen helped us to victory during the Battle of Britain. After the war it was reopened briefly for civil aviation usage and there were regular flights to London, but the last remaining building had the remnants of Second World War weapons-training rotas still on the walls. Now long demolished, it is here that the ghost of a Polish airman in full flying combat kit is supposed to have been seen, and in the early 1980s was said to still frequent the site.

On the outskirts of Hartlepool is the cosy, sleepy village of Elwick. At the rustic pub, The McOrville, representatives from *Paranormal Magazine* joined a team of local mediums and ghost hunters for a vigil and exploration which began at noon on a Saturday and ended at 6 a.m. on the Sunday in early 2006. Supposed contact was made with a young boy, tables moved

With a century of occupancy and twenty rooms, The Douglas Hotel has a record of regular paranormal activity and has attracted commercial vigils. The day the author called, the housekeeper had heard a discarnate woman's voice just before a glass for orange juice shattered into smithereens. (© Paul Screeton)

Publicity for Elwick's McOrville pub includes stories of its resident ghost. (© Paul Screeton)

around and 'orbs' (more of which anon) were captured on film. Several local residents were observers, and landlord Darren Holmes got into the spirit of the enterprise and afterwards told *Hartlepool Mail* reporter Karen Faughey: 'We made contact with a 5-year-old boy named Gus, who says he died here around sixty-seven years ago. There was a feeling that he was probably killed by a horse.' I must admit to having my reservations about several aspects of this account. How do spirits measure time? Also, a horse connection with the pub's name is a giveaway; consciously or subconsciously it could have been known that the pub is named after a racehorse which was stabled and trained on a local farm and was famed for its exploits on courses in the locality long ago. McOrville denotes 'son of Orville'

(not Scots origin), Orville being the renowned winner of the St Leger in 1802. Dating from the seventeenth century, the pub was formerly named the Fox and Hounds.

As for orbs, these are generally bright circular anomalies within an image, appearing singly or in multiple, and of varying colour and intensity. During my research for this book, a number of people showed me photographs with circular objects which they deemed to be supernatural. But the evolution in digital imaging, beginning in the 1990s, perfectly tracked the rise in claims for orbs by ghost hunters, while sceptics strove to prove that airborne material located close to the camera and reflecting the camera flash is responsible for creating orbs. Perhaps the jury is still out on this one?

Well, we all have to go, and the figure of a priest has been spotted in The Causeway toilet. (© Paul Screeton)

However, I also came across a variation on the theme. Described as a 'purple upside down jellyfish', a baffling object was caught on video camera by ghost hunters probing the supernatural in the ancient Stranton pub The Causeway. The bizarre floating apparition was recorded in the cellar, where landlady Thelma Adams had felt uneasy until telling the unpleasant presence to desist. It has apparently done so, but patrons have seen the figure of a priest in the toilet of the modern extension. This has been speculated as belonging to All Saints church next door and there's the ubiquitous tunnel legend. On a personal level, whenever the paranormal is mentioned, sceptical Thelma breaks out in goosepimples.

Few places in England have as rich a history and heritage as the charming picture postcard village of Hart, on the outskirts of Hartlepool. Its ancient pedigree dates back to Anglo-Saxon times, since when there has been a lingering local legend that here stood a great mead hall dispensing drunkenness and debauchery under the tutelage of the bold Beowulf. The eponymous poem detailing the warrior's derring-do is the earliest heroic epic saga in the English language. Some say it is set in Scandinavia, but we have to thank Father Daniel Henry Haigh, who located the great hall in Hart and uncovered the monster-slaying feat in a Hartlepool area formerly known as The Slake, subsequently drained to create the successful port. Scholars have tended to dismiss Father Haigh as a fanciful amateur with a partisan agenda. Danish king Hrothgar's palace was deemed fantasy – that was until aerial photography pinpointed the foundation posts and pattern of a huge rectangular wooden structure so Haigh's theory was dusted off (but never universally accepted).

Then there was Robert the Bruce. The Scottish hero was the eighth member of the Brus lineage to be named Robert, owned estates in Scotland and was also the Lord of Heortness, covering Hart and Hartlepool. He boldly canvassed his claim to the Scottish throne and in his efforts became involved with the spider legend, whereby the creature's dogged efforts inspired him and spurred him on to realise his ambition. Thus Scotsmen are reluctant to kill spiders. He was born in Hart itself – well, that's the legend.

Hart Vicarage, dating from the pre-Georgian era, has the familiar Grey Lady. A former occupant of the parsonage told of her having spoken with him on several occasions: a young woman dressed in Victorian-era clothing who sat by his fireside. The plaintive perambulating of a man in a frock coat and top hat has also been sighted, in secluded Butts Lane. He is believed to be the remorseful spirit of a former vicar, who refused a tramp his request for alms. The vagrant subsequently hanged himself in the adjacent stables. The clergyman still walks his familiar haunts and, if local people are to be believed, the vagabond too has been seen occasionally. Perhaps if they were to meet one another the matter could be resolved amicably, which could mean two fewer ethereal characters in this cauldron of mysteries.

Despite having collected local ghost-lore all my adult life, the tales I have to tell regarding St Mary Magdalene church were all new to me. Their compiler is even younger than I was when I first became interested as a teenager, for Harriet Colledge was at the time

Another Grey Lady is one of numerous ghosts associated with Hart Vicarage. (© Paul Screeton)

Hart's ancient St Mary Magdalene church's vestry is a focus for paranormal activity. (© Paul Screeton)

a 10-year-old member of St Joseph's R.C. Primary School Research Club. She shone a spotlight on Hart's ancient church, with its architectural contributions from many eras, dating from the Anglo-Saxon. As for the supernatural, the focus would seem to be the vestry and when workmen were restoring the church, if they made a noise, a corresponding droning sound would be emitted from the vestry. In a similar fashion, if a living person shouted, it was claimed the ghost would shout back. Not only is the vestry supposed to be abnormally cold, but when people have stood close by they have heard voices chanting and moving slowly towards the vestry door.

Hart Windmill is not a modern electricity-generating eyesore, but a recently renovated, old-fashioned grain grinder. It began production in 1314 and corn was ground here for six centuries until 1915, when the last sack of flour was produced. The mill is reputedly haunted by a miller's wife − a transient image, which develops into the vexed subject of disappearing family snapshots. Of course newspaper photographers always enjoy the opportunity to show their skills at trick photography with double exposure. Illustrating ghost stories offers a challenge to produce a facsimile similar to what the witness has described at that very spot. Naturally there have been many deliberate fabrications to deceive for either financial gain or sheer devilment. In this instance there is a claim that in the 1970s an unidentified person took a Polaroid shot outside the twelfth-century mill. There standing to one side of the couple he had snapped was a white figure. Forteans are familiar with the phenomenon of vital evidence having a regular habit of disappearing before serious investigation can be made into its genuineness. In this hazy – already para-normal – case, unfortunately the picture was lost before photographic experts could examine it.

Visitors to Hart cannot but be impressed by the ship's figurehead on the façade of The White Hart. The lady in question is from the sailing barque *Rising Sun*, one of sixty ships wrecked in Hartlepool Bay by the great storm of 1861. More recently, time spent in this pub by me goes back to early courting days in the 1960s, but in 2012 I sat in a corner of the bar where a door leads to the toilets and was told this was the haunt of shadowy figures which have not been seen elsewhere in the pub. I was told this gastronomic haven has cold spots in summer, doors slam of their own accord and wine glasses have an expensive habit of falling from shelves. I was also informed that a Hallowe'en vigil around four years previously 'proved positive', but no details or record appear forthcoming. I have no idea of the date for the building, but the name may be of pagan origin for the white hart symbolised the Old Religion, represented by a man wearing horns and sometimes the head of a stag.

The Raby Arms is nicknamed the 'Bottom House' to distinguish it from the previous pub being the 'Top House'. The spook here is somewhat more substantial, said to be a nurse from the days when the popular family-oriented pub was a hospital. Subsequently it was a school and then a post office. The nurse again morphs into that catch-all Grey Lady in local lore and it is she who is blamed if patrons feel a sudden chill in the corridor outside the toilets, and not a draught from the back door, for it is claimed that even in summertime this passageway is icy cold.

Hart's Grey Lady also pops down to the Raby Arms. (© Paul Screeton)

Lastly in Hart, a sharp bend in Butts Lane – where this ramble around idyllic Hart began – is known locally as the Devil's Elbow. Those familiar with the more esoteric levels of earth mysteries research will appreciate the mystique attached to places with 'Devil' in the name as being associated with evidence (or otherwise) of special numinosity in the environs and a liminality between the natural and supernatural landscapes.

During the Cold War, huge radio scanners were positioned between Tees Road and Brenda Road, Hartlepool, lying on rough pastureland. If they weren't easy enough to spot by aerial photography, also above ground was the guardroom, an identikit brick building. Known in Spies for Peace lingo as a 'decoy farmhouse', these buildings were a giveaway across the country to enemy agents as all were identical architecturally and signified the entrance to 'secret' underground bunker networks. The example along Brenda Road was demolished relatively recently, the operations room below to monitor any Russian nuclear strike having long been abandoned after technology overtook the site's usefulness as RAF Seaton Snook. Instead the radar 'mushrooms' and latterly more sophisticated 'pyramid' at Fylingdales have sprung up to protect us from the perceived 'Red Menace'.

Hartlepool Mail correspondent Colin Draper, of Kirkstone Drive, Hartlepool, had a couple of letters published in 1998 referring to his service at the radar station and setting other commentators straight. He asked if anyone had information about a burial ground on the bend of Tees Road where it meets Brenda Road, which was then flat but is now the site of a huge waste tip. The point he made, which should interest us here, regards the well-attested ability of animals to react to supernatural phenomena. I'll let him take up the thread:

When we were on fire picket patrol, we slept at the site and during the daylight hours we would help the RAF Police to train the Alsatians. We would be asked to run towards the corner mentioned above, with padded arm protection, the dogs would chase us and bring us down. However, when we got within sixty yards of the boundary fence, the dogs would not chase us across an imaginary line. If the RAF dog handler took the dog in his arms, the dog would leap out when the invisible line was reached and would not obey any order to go to him when he stood on the 'burial ground'. I have made extensive inquiries into this and only one person knew anything about it. It appears that a plague in 1880-90 killed about 450 people, who were buried in a mass grave there.

I can neither verify nor challenge this notion, but 'plague pit' references, often of dubious provenance, have frustrated historians with the vagueness with which they are claimed. This motif has also clouded folklore and in particular is viewed with great suspicion by contemporary legend collectors. Tales are told with wild abandon that curves on the London Underground exist where trains are detoured to avoid plague pits. Naturally, there have been well-documented plagues, but any historian or folklorist will warn that you are treading on dodgy ground!

Back to the theme of psychic animals and another local angle, the Bombardment of Hartlepool marked the first loss of a serviceman's life on British soil during

The Heugh Battery, on the Headland, is still patrolled by a phantom soldier. (© Paul Screeton)

In Hartlepool's Stranton Cemetery at 2 p.m. on 30 September 1988, Olga Smith was tending her mother's grave when she witnessed a small but fierce whirlwind, which she chose to call an 'angry spirit' lifting leaves, flowers and even pots into the air. The localised phenomenon lasted for little more than a minute, disturbing what had been absolute calm. Another observer even likened it to a tornado. (© Paul Screeton)

the First World War. It is rumoured that as First Lord of the Admiralty, Winston Churchill was aware of German battle cruisers intending to fire upon the ports of Scarborough, Whitby and the Hartlepools, but did not wish to let the enemy know British Intelligence was aware of their every intention. My late father told me as a child, when visiting the local museum, how hours before the *Blücher*, *Moltke* and *Seydlitz* hove into view, all the dogs and cats in the twin towns streamed off into the safety of the countryside. Their seeking shelter towards Hart, Elwick and Dalton Piercy is again familiar territory to me as a folklorist, for there is voluminous evidence of all manner of wildlife reacting to future events of which we un-attuned humans have no contact.

The First World War shelling of the Hartlepools could have been avoided had the gun at the Headland's Heugh Battery not been impeded by a lighthouse positioned between it and the enemy warships. Today, the battery has been renovated and can be visited. It is rumoured to be haunted by a soldier who patrols the grounds, particularly at night. Could it be the shade of the first serviceman to die on British soil during that conflict? It has been the scene of at least one ghost-hunting vigil and also a visit by Ralph Keeton, who has appeared on TV's *Most Haunted*. The medium, who has organised Headland paid-for ghost walks for the public, claims he engaged separately two long-departed nuns on one of these excursions. The second encounter was with a sister who had been brutally murdered and occurred in the Friarage gardens. Could she have been the phantom Grey Lady we met in several other locations on the Headland earlier?

TWO

SCARY SPOOKS

GRANDMOTHERS are traditionally saintly, caring people, full of goodwill and wisdom, having raised a family, that dote on and spoil rotten their grandchildren. But one particular old woman was rotten in life and even worse in death, who even her family utterly disowned. A sozzled old soak, when she passed away she found a warped pleasure in terrorising her daughter's offspring. The gruesome ghostly granny from Hell terrorised the Frobisher family [all names with respect to the troubled family have been changed to protect their privacy] in their Hutton Avenue, Hartlepool, home. For eighteen tiring years, the old woman's daughter Gemma and her husband John looked after alcoholic and diabetic Gladys in their home, but eventually their patience was at the end of their tether and they finally put the bad-tempered boozer in an old people's home. Within six months she was dead, aged 69, but spitefully returned to get her revenge in spirit form. Upon first seeing her as an apparition, Ian registered mainly a mist, 'but the shadow was unmistakeable as she scowled and staggered towards me. I ran away petrified and in a cold sweat.'

Gemma, too, had encounted the old woman's spirit. She recalled to a newspaper reporter how they had responded:

We thought we were each going mad, but later found out we had both been seeing the same thing. We saw her walking along the hall and she looked exactly the same as when she was alive. She was the kind of woman to play mental games and really wasn't your stereotype gran. I might have known she would do this. She wasn't really a nice woman. Although we took her in and looked after her, she resented it. But when the children first complained she was appearing in their bedroom I thought 'enough is enough', I don't want my children involved.

The soused spirit returned a dozen times until Gemma finally snapped when her mother put her icy hand on her. 'You could see the imprint on my back and it was as if a hand carved of ice had touched me. I turned around and shouted at her, "After everything I've done for you, you ungrateful cow. Leave us alone." We haven't seen her since.' That was during the period when the less-than-Super Gran focussed her evil attention on the unfortunate grandchildren, 4-year-old Rose and Lily, aged 6. They would wake up and scream as their grandmother hovered at the end of their bed, pulling ugly faces to scare them. At this stage the couple called upon the services of a priest, who blessed each room with holy water. Investigating the case for his book on hauntings, psychic sleuth Francis Marshall states that neighbours related to him how a smell like being in a pub pervaded the house every Sunday – but the Frobishers were teetotal.

As a folklorist, contemporary legend (or as it is popularly known, urban myth) has been my forte and the tale attached to former Cabinet Minister Peter Mandelson of mistaking mushy peas for avocado mousse in a Seaton Carew fish and chips shop has been recycled umpteen times. I wrote a book of local humorous and bizarre tales entitled *The Man Who Ate a Domino* and after publicity in the *Hartlepool Mail* (I had just taken early retirement to concentrate on freelance writing), I received a phone call that night from a chilly voice asking where they could buy a copy most easily. I told the anonymous voice that Atkinson Print was selling copies on my behalf and the disembodied voice rang off. If that had been meant to be a friendly inquiry, I can imagine the terror and panic it would strike into anyone who knew he or she had offended the Darth Vader of Westminster. An even more complete history of the guacamole meme appears in my analysis of modern folklore, *Mars Bar & Mushy Peas*.

A newspaper report claimed: 'A council used taxpayers' money to get a psychic to perform an exorcism at a house where locals say a man murdered his wife 50 years ago.' It was a three-bedroom council house in Peterlee, but accounts failed to name the street. Despite the *Daily Telegraph*'s grisly claim, the tenants, Sabrina and Martin Fallon, came to believe a child was responsible for the haunting. A not unfamiliar element to such tales is that they begin with noises in the loft and in this instance 23-year-old Mrs Fallon called the police at 5.30 one morning, fearing intruders. Nothing was found, but one of the officers remarked: 'Have you

The urban legend which haunts Peter Mandelson: did he mistake mushy peas for avocado mousse? The Dark Lord as visualised in a local 'chippie' by cartoonist Paul Jermy. The illustration originally appeared in this author's self-published humorous book The Man Who Ate a Domino.

ever thought that you had a ghost?' Well, no she hadn't, but then she saw the figure of a small girl sitting on the stairs (a very liminal place) with her head bowed.

The Fallons had two young children, Amie (aged 1) and Shannon (9), and the former was to feature in a critical episode in a mounting series of incidents. When Amie's bedroom door suddenly closed of its own volition, Mrs Fallon began to panic and told how: 'I thought, I have to get Amie out. I tried Amie's door and it was as if it were jammed'. She finally wrenched it open only to find the child safe but the room icy cold despite the heating being on.

Physically, this sounds like a typical poltergeist, as the couple also suspected. According to a version of events written by Danny Penman:

> Objects flew through the air, furniture inexplicably moved of its own accord and the family was subjected to the relentless sound of whispering and banging in their loft. On one occasion, they saw a nightie float through the air. On another, the ghostly figure of a young girl walked across the landing.

Mrs Fallon added that in addition to coldness despite the heating being turned on, the house 'was dull no matter how bright the lights were and there was a horrid smell. It was like living in a mortuary.' As for the medium, she was 35-year-old Suzanne Hadwin, who charged £120, half of which was controversially met from council funds. Contacted by Mrs Fallon to perform an exorcism, according to one report the professional psychic did not visit personally. Instead, as Sabrina recalled:

> She sent her spiritual guide to the house. Me being me, I was waiting for a knock at the door. We got a call back later that night from Suzanne [who] didn't even know that I had two children, let alone their names. She knew everything – even the colour of the walls in our home. She said this male figure wanted to possess my daughter's body in order to relive his life. His name was Peter and he was a poltergeist.

Suzanne was convinced her investigation had erased the evil presence from the house and Mrs Fallon seemed no longer afraid to remain in her home. A spokesman for the council said, 'This is the first time we have had to take such action. However, the tenants were pleased with the outcome.'

Alan Murdie's synthesis of the case in *Fortean Times* is somewhat at odds with the above and the little girl scenario. His has the medium making an initial visit bodily, followed by Mrs Fallon being assaulted physically by an unseen presence trying to wrench Amie (or as Penman has it, Amy) from her arms and leaving red marks on her shoulder (shades of physical skin damage as in the Hutton Avenue encounter above). 'It was the first time my husband believed me,' and it was in another account how the 24-year-old quit his lorry-driving job to protect his family, and who was later told that fifty years previously a man had murdered his wife on the landing with a poker and subsequently hanged himself. As for whether the council's largesse should have stretched to paying a ghostbuster, Alan Murdie points out that Brighton and Hove District Council appointed the 'secular exorcist' Andrew Green as a consultant 'surveyor' of supposedly haunted properties.

Imaginary friends or 'quasi-corporeal companions', Hartlepool's Belmont Gardens had visitors from another dimension. (© Paul Screeton)

In Hartlepool, an intriguing case from Belmont Gardens comes sneaking into this loose category as it involves an adult couple's unease, although the ones in the family who were interacting with a phenomenon were children, who believed they had the good fortune to have found a playmate already resident in their new home. The story begins in the 1970s, with a letter to a newspaper. In the year of the Queen's Silver Jubilee, wrote the correspondent, neighbourly acquaintanceships were strengthened and new friendships forged. Responding to an article about ghosts in homes in the *Property Today* supplement, where readers were invited to share their experiences, the writer recalled that during the planning for a street party he made friends with the couple who lived opposite and whose children were the same age as

his. Chatting over coffee, mention was made of a haunting there and the mother explained how her children were visited by the ghost of a young boy, with whom they played in their bedroom. The storyteller – who asked for anonymity for themself and that of the address where the incidents took place – moved away in the 1980s and thought no more about the supernatural claim until a few years ago when a new colleague joined his place of work. He had a young family, had just moved into Belmont Gardens and – yes – his brood was receiving nocturnal visits from a spectral pal. No surprise, it was the very same house as previously.

This tale from the *Hartlepool Mail* is a familiar yet little researched aspect of ghostlore, if that is not to compartmentalise the phenomenon unfairly. Certainly if it was repeating itself with decades in between, it is unlikely two families' children would have identical over-imaginative impulses to create an invisible (at least to adults) friend. North East paranormalist and author Mike Hallowell has written a book on the subject in response to his disbelief that although roughly one-third of children claim to have or had an imaginary childhood friend, this widespread phenomenon had been basically overlooked by paranormalists and forteans in general. Naturally, it has not been neglected by child psychologists, who work from the assumption that it is merely a phase in the growing-up process. Mike's approach has not been the psychological one, whereby it is reduced to being the positive expression of individual imagination or on a darker level an indication of impending dissociative disorders, but seeing the imaginary friend as helping those so visited to hone social skills and achieve behavioural stability. I applaud Mike for going out on a limb to dismiss the term 'imaginary childhood friends' as meaningless. Mike argues that 'imaginary' can be discarded as they have a form of 'real' existence; also 'childhood' is restricting and unhelpful in adult encounters (such as the greatest psychologist of all, Carl Gustav Jung, and his confederate Philemon), and 'friends' fails to correctly describe their rather quixotic relationship and behaviour towards true humanity and abnormal playmate activities. Instead, Mike calls them 'quasi-corporeal companions (Q-CCs)', which I think is both clever and accurate. Perhaps now is the time to bring Q-CCs in from the realm of the subjective and elaborate childish fantasies and treat them in an adult fashion by awarding them the respect visitors from another dimension deserve.

On a totally different tack, the anonymous former Belmont Gardens tenant's letter also draws attention to another debateable point: whether the presence of a ghost adds or subtracts from a property's value. Certainly historic buildings and pubs of a certain age benefit from a claimed link to the spirit world beyond whisky, gin and vodka in their CVs; but does your average housing property? A rum do to be sure. In fact, contrary to general belief, as with bad neighbours, estate agencies don't tell potential buyers about any supernatural manifestations. Statistically, one in ten householders think their house is haunted and according to a Hallowe'en property survey by Yorkshire Bank Mortgages in 2007, more than half of all house hunters would be willing to make an offer if the property was rumoured to have a resident ghost. In fact, one in three would be even keener to make a viewing. As we have seen only too clearly presented here, in very rare cases supernatural intervention can be disturbing rather than dinner party small talk or a subject for conversation around a bar-room table. Yorkshire Bank's Garry Lumby warned would-be house-buyers: 'We all know to look out for damp patches and cracks in the walls when viewing a home, but it could prove trickier to spot a supernatural problem with your potential property.' *Caveat emptor!*

It can be hard enough to get children to go to school, never mind return in their free time, but on 21 June 1973 an estimated 200–300 pupils had to be removed from the grounds of Peterlee's Dene House School by police. This voluntary return was in the nature of a ghost-hunting escapade. Somehow a rumour had spread that a haunting would occur visibly in the library at 7.30 p.m. Earlier in the week, talk had circulated of sightings of a nun standing over a pool of blood. One version stated that her throat was cut. She then became known as 'Mary' (Bloody Mary perhaps?) Another addition to the tale was that she met her untimely end in a nunnery over whose foundations the school was rumoured to be built. As the legend grew it was claimed her grave in a nearby cemetery was open. Then it was stated that a teacher had spotted the spook in a stock cupboard.

By the time the police ushered the pupils away, a revised version was circulating: that the spectre was a former resident of a cottage over which the school was alleged to stand. And there the tale might have died. However, a Mr Don Leslie, then aged 68 and living in Hutton Henry, remembered Dene House Farm, where he formerly lived, and recalled that it was close to the school complex. His comments are certainly apposite in the light of the pupils' insistence of something untoward having an association with the place. Mr Leslie recalled:

> One night after my wife and I had gone to bed I asked her if she had let the cat in. We heard noises on the sideboard. Then I heard footsteps coming up the stairs and they stopped outside the bedroom. I got up and had a look around, but there wasn't anyone to be seen. There was definitely something there. We did not tell many people about this in case it frightened them away.

A relation who frequently stayed at the farm referred to the phenomenon as 'the gentleman'. Mr Leslie also recalled a young Polish family who made a quick departure because they were uneasy about the place's atmosphere. 'We had horses at the farm and one night I saw them listening to something and they were very uneasy,' he said. 'They were staring as if they had seen something strange. On another occasion I was told that a woman had once hung [sic] a dog from a tree. The farm was almost 300 years old and it wouldn't surprise me if it hadn't been the scene of many strange deeds. There was something disturbing about the farm.'

This tale certainly has the merit of having substance. In the twenty-first century it seems both similar to the internet-inspired 'flash mob' phenomenon, plus largely American experience of students 'legend tripping' or believing 'campus rumours', usually associated with potential gun slayings or malevolent street gangs about to rape the female students.

A single schoolboy figures in a terrifying tale which stands out as it is the only one here to feature an invisible assailant in a starring role. Teenager Daniel Wilkins made headlines in national newspapers in July 2009 when he claimed he was attacked in his home during one afternoon. The *Hartlepool Mail* headline proclaimed 'Boy beaten up by ghost', and reporting on the incident in the *Fortean Times*, Alan Murdie noted: 'While tactile experiences seem to make up around 12 per cent of ghost reports, they are seldom as violent as this one.'

It was not a happy Monday for the 13 year old when he was sitting alone listening to music on the sofa in rented accommodation in York Road, Hartlepool. He said he was suddenly pulled upright, dragged across the living room and into the kitchen. Purportedly, a titanic struggle lasting all of five minutes ensued, culminating in the front door suddenly flying open and Daniel being pushed into the street by the invisible intruder. Out of the house, it seems the lad was free from the presence and he fled to a neighbour's house. Described as being left 'bruised and bewildered' by the encounter, he recalled that he saw nothing, but heard a man's heavy breathing. While this was going on, Daniel's mother, 33-year-old Beverley, had been collecting a younger son and on her return found Daniel on the doorstep, trembling. They entered the house with trepidation but fled upon hearing footsteps and banging from upstairs. That night, they returned and huddled together in one bedroom, but were disturbed and spooked by a fire alarm being repeatedly activated. The vicar of St Paul's church, Father Richard Masshedar, was contacted and he gave comfort and offered prayers in the house. Assuming events in the accounts were as reported, Daniel experienced the rare incidence of a particularly violent invisible assailant. Poltergeists are generally regarded as mischievous rather than malevolent and this unseen presence was a danger to life and limb.

In nearby Milton Road, single parent and father-of-three Bob Coxon was so spooked by happenings while renting his home that he delayed turning in for the night:

I only feel safe going to bed after 1.30 a.m. Between 11.15 p.m. well into midnight is when the disturbances start up. I have heard footsteps going up and down the fire escape, but when I've investigated there's no one there. One night this week I went out to check and even as I stood there I could hear the steps. When I looked up at the house I saw a face at the window of a room that is never used.

It was then he heard a voice crying out, 'Help me, please help me.' But he was the only person there. Neighbours recalled a raging fire that swept through the house twenty to twenty-five years previously which claimed the lives of a number of children from a large family living there. Mysterious occurrences began shortly after Mr Coxon moved in and there was footsteps in empty rooms. He hoped somehow to lay 'the ghost' to rest.

A former Hartlepool cinema warrants a brief mention, having been the scene of a workman terrified upon waking at the end of a night-time shift refurbishing the bar when the premises was a Fair World bingo club in 1976. All the *Hartlepool Mail* could reveal was that he was called Martin and came from Bradford. His landlady, Mrs Rachel Saddler, of Hartlepool Avenue, Horden, was more forthcoming and quoted as saying Martin 'came home one morning white as a sheet and obviously very frightened. He said he had been asleep at the end of his shift, but something had woken him up. When he opened his eyes, he told me saw an apparition dancing in front of him.' She added that Martin had seen the ghost several times in the intervening period, which would discount a hypnopompic illusion. 'It's got to the state now where he won't sleep in the place and is even reluctant to go to work at night. He's a sensible lad and I don't think he would make this up.' A vague epilogue to the story records a Wolviston resident called Jimmy Mincher, who as a boy fell asleep at the end of a screening and found he was locked in. While seeking his way out he witnessed a phantom, although there are no further details.

Latterly Hartlepool Snooker and Social Club, the former cinema premises are currently vacant – except for a resident ghost. (© Paul Screeton)

Now for a complete change of scenery. Where the footbridge crosses the A19 near Norton Mill you can sense tension, even in the daytime air. At present it is frustration emanating from hundreds of drivers in traffic jams centred upon Billingham Bottoms roundabout. Maybe at night when there are far fewer cars it is different. Or worse? For here once stood Norton Mill, reputedly haunted by a total of three ghosts.

At one time the mill owner was a man called Gossack. His medical student son was always up to pranks. He had hidden a human skeleton in a dark corner of the mill and when a young maidservant came upon it, the shock was sufficient for her to die raving mad from fright. The girl's father was grief-stricken, laid in wait for the miller – whom he blamed for his son's stupid jape – killed him with an axe and hid the body near the mill. The murderer was found guilty and hanged, but supposedly Gossack remained in spectral form to terrorise the place which had once been his home. Legend avers that he regularly scared unsuspecting wayfarers in the lanes around the mill. With flashing eyes and a leering grin he would suddenly appear, before departing with a mocking, 'Goodnight'. So terrifying was he that few people in the locality would venture near the mill at night.

Yet the mill's two earlier spooks were even more eerie. There was a bloodstained phantom hand grasping a fiendish knife which allegedly floated from room to room, as if in search of a victim. There was also a luminous, grinning head of a white-haired woman, which was said to closely follow the hand. Her head dripped blood and her eyes were forever darting anxiously, as if seeking a way of escape. It seems the origin of the earlier phantoms has been lost forever, but it is alleged that Gossack himself, before his murder, often talked of them in fearful tones. For him to later haunt the same vicinity puts an ironic twist to the tale of a triple haunting.

THREE

PUB SPIRITS

KNOWING that my wife and I enjoy pub lunches on my day off, when a new column reviewing licensed premises which served food was mooted I was first choice. This column on pub grub, ale and ambience became known as 'Pub Spy' – a popular Saturday feature in the *Hartlepool Mail*. To make conversation, I would sometimes ask landlords or bar staff if there was a resident ghost and include it in the review. Of course, when drumming up trade it makes good sense to spice it up with an added – and free – attraction. Only trouble is, does the tale peddle a pedigree or was it manufactured to drum up business? It has been said that publicising the presence of a troubled spirit on licensed premises has been a publican's ruse since pagan times and I can believe it.

So, off down the pub, and where more appropriate than where all this paranormal interest began for me, Hartlepool's own White House. Here I believe I may have had a low-key supernatural encounter when young. I was around 10 years old and one of four pupils from

the since-demolished Elwick Road Junior School, passing in darkness what was then an unoccupied but prestigious house in several acres of grounds at the junction of Grange and Wooler Roads. It became St Francis Xavier School and eventually a licensed premises with more tangible spirits, the White House, so named for its perceived resemblance to the official residence of presidents of the United States of America.

In the 1950s, youngsters had little else to do for amusement on an evening but wander the darkened streets in aimless fashion. So this particular evening we found ourselves passing the overgrown frontage of what had been a mansion named Normanhurst. Out of the four of us, another boy and I witnessed what appeared to be a wispy white shape of human dimensions, 'drifting' in front of the decaying house. Upon retelling this incident as a sixth-former at West Hartlepool Grammar School, a fellow student related that he too had been in the grounds of the house around this period and had seen a hand hanging out of an

Hartlepool's own presidential-style gastropub, The White House. Before its current incarnation, an experience here triggered the author's interest in the paranormal. (© Paul Screeton)

upstairs window. Somewhat concerned, but suspecting it could be attached to some tramp, he entered with trepidation, but a thorough search failed to reveal any human presence. While researching this book, I heard a story that in either the cellar or the loft there were beds from when the house was commandeered as an emergency hospital for First World War wounded, but manager Dave McCann assured me the cellar is only for beer kegs and the loft has been insulated and used for storage (but not beds). He thought the rumour could have originated from the previous manageress who would tell tall stories to amuse children.

If the White House had a role to play in fostering my interest in the paranormal, Hartlepool's Jacksons Arms played a role in wrapping up a long career in journalism. Here I held my leaving do. But in all those years and subsequently I never felt anything spooky about the place. Named after its chief shareholder,

Ralph Ward Jackson, he and associates planned this street corner boozer to be upmarket when West Hartlepool was growing fast and Jackson wanted a place where fellow businessman would not feel intimidated by the lower classes and prostitutes. By the time of its construction, Jackson had deliberately distanced himself from the pubs in Mainsforth Terrace, already nicknamed the 'Barbary Coast'. It even had – and has – a Saracen's head above the doorway (until recently it had been caringly painted in correct colours for its subject, but is now uniformly black along with the remainder of the doorway); no doubt designed to act as a guardian. Unlike Seaton Carew's Station Hotel's protective heads (discussed later), I do not think true evil is involved. Riff-raff, rogues and harlots over the years will have spoiled Jackson's dream, but today it is a more peaceable establishment, although the Saracen's head has not deterred the spirit world.

Above the Jacksons Arms' entrance is a figurative head. Perhaps Saracen or Turk? It's a Freemasons' symbol and Marie-Louise McKay told me that Camerons Brewery is replete with such Masonic signs, if you know what to look for. (© Paul Screeton)

When local medium Peter Crawford made a commercial DVD, *Haunted Hartlepool*, he found plenty of evidence in various pubs for activity from the 'other side'. He told the *Hartlepool Mail*:

> It was fascinating to take part and the Jacksons Arms, in Tower Street, was the most haunted. The first thing I saw was a lady with bleached blonde hair who looked like a lady of the night. When I told a few of the regulars what I'd seen, they knew who it was straight away and were really astounded.

A well-known Diana Dors lookalike, I immediately recognised her from the description, too. And the corner where the hookers were seated in spirit is notorious for minor incidents, such as persons glimpsed who were not actually there and drinks being spilled. Landlord Trevor Wilding's previous German shepherd Sasha would not go near the corner.

Trevor witnessed a glass shooting off a non-slip shelf opposite and the medium described a girl ghost responsible for mischief, such as touching barmaids, and the child told Peter Crawford she liked the pink bed socks Trevor's wife had been wearing early one morning. Andrea Wilding's brother, Kevin Mallinson, had seen the shade of another girl, one in her late teens, while changing a barrel in the cellar and one of the regular draymen is so scared of the cellar he always remains at the top of the steps handing stock to his mate below.

Around the corner in Church Square – and named after the same man – is the Ward Jackson. This classy gastropub, formerly a bank, now has an all-glass frontage giving a splendid view of the eccentric architecture of Christ Church and statue of West Hartlepool founder Ralph Ward Jackson himself. I began to experience odd phenomena here in 2012 when around 10 a.m. one day

The statue of Ralph Ward Jackson outside the spooky Ward Jackson pub itself. (© Paul Screeton)

I was passing and noticed my favourite alcove was occupied by a middle-aged blonde woman, obscuring a companion, and staring at me. In fact, this was so strange that I checked I had not been seeing things as clientele are rare so early – and the semi-circular booth was empty. No one could have passed me! A week or so later, again 'early doors', I spotted a woman with brown hair in the same spot as I passed. Inspection revealed no one was there. Then, on 11 January 2013, there were two women occupying seats in the alcove as I passed and I thought the clutter of shopping on the table and floor at 10 a.m. very odd. Again it had been a phantom sighting. Manager Lindsay McConnell had no explanation or heard of any other ghostly reports.

As a seaport, Hartlepool naturally has a seagoing spectre. His berth is now The Royal, a Regency-style edifice facing what was Hartlepool's original town centre when built in the mid-1840s. Generations of drinkers have known it as 'The Royal Back', as the entrance is around the corner in Lower Church Street from the grand yellow-brick frontage. When new tenants created an upmarket restaurant in 1981, they named it the Captain's Cabin after stories they heard from regulars that the former junk room they had made shipshape was haunted by a seafaring captain. Farther inland, in Murray Street, the local branch of the Royal Naval Association (everyone calls it 'The Navy Club'), also has a resident spirit, but despite the name it's not some salty old sea dog. The presence has been named Annie, after a regular patron who lived next door before passing on. A committee member who was sorting bingo books upstairs had an unnerving experience which left him in no doubt that the randy wraith had made him an unearthly indecent proposal.

Along the coast in Seaton Carew is a pub we will meet again, although it was demolished a few years ago. The very last landlady, Brenda Farrow, was told by two separate spiritualist mediums giving readings at the Station Hotel that the nineteenth-century pub was haunted by two children who had lived at the top of the building in the servants' quarters. They were named William and Elizabeth. Brenda's daughter-in-law Candice stayed overnight and her daughter India could not settle and was 'petrified' while there. It was she who had attracted the spirit of Elizabeth and when India returned home she was accompanied by Elizabeth. After a period of receiving no attention, the child-ghost supposedly returned to the doomed pub.

Dating from the era when stage-coaches changed horses while travellers took refreshments, the former stables often have a legend of a person hanging themselves there. The frequency of the theme gives it the tenor of what folklorists name a migratory legend, a branch of urban myth. Latterly a home for the elderly, the Kirkham was popular for its vista across Hartlepool Bay in its days as a hostelry. In addition to a boy found hanging from the rafters, who supposedly haunts the Headland house, anecdotal evidence links it to the presence of a girl raped and murdered in Middleham, North Yorkshire.

Named after a vessel, The Royal boasts a seagoing captain as resident spirit. (© Paul Screeton)

Not a former mariner as might be expected, but a departed patron named Annie spooked a committee man at 'The Navy Club'. (© Paul Screeton)

When in use as a pub, The Kirkham was supposedly haunted by a boy who hanged himself. (© Paul Screeton)

A hanging in stables also features in the history of the Castle Eden inn, a village pub with an international claim to fame. It was here that the very first friendly – or benefit – society was inaugurated in the pub in 1793. As for the ghost at this popular eatery, he is decidedly unfriendly. The stables where he hanged himself are an area now occupied by the function room, and people have reported a sensation of being strangled or choked within the inn. There are also accounts of a woman looking despairingly from an upper window in Castle Eden's only pub.

From horses, hangings and alcohol, to cars, a showroom and more ale now. The wine bar chain Yates's is represented in Hartlepool with a branch opened in 1997 in Victoria Road. Another gastropub, it had at one time been a car showroom with workshops at the rear. Supposedly,

during the time it was Gales's Garage, a mechanic was working underneath a car when the jack holding it up collapsed and the worker was fatally injured. His spirit lives on, however, and members of staff have reported being touched by an unseen presence when down the cellar.

Over on Hartlepool's Headland there is a statue commemorating the town's most famous 'son'. Not only is the honoured gentleman an anti-hero, but he has only ever existed as a cartoon character. The loveable rogue Andy Capp looks out across Hartlepool Bay, leaning nonchalantly with a pint beside him on the bar. I mention Andy because witnesses of two sightings of paranormal activity likened what they saw to the cartoon character. It is almost like Andy so embodies the spirit of Hartlepool that his comic-strip persona is manifesting, as if having a

The façade of the Castle Eden Inn hides the fact it was the birthplace of friendly societies, yet has a distinctly unfriendly ghost. (© Paul Screeton)

At Yates's Hartlepool wine bar the spirit of a mechanic has taken up residence in the cellar. (© Paul Screeton)

An Andy Capp-style spectre has been spotted in the Victoria Arms, Hartlepool. (© Paul Screeton)

quasi-existence in the afterlife! First it was in The Brunswick (latterly renamed with the pseudo-historic title Victoria Arms). Former landlord Colin Eglintine told me that when he ran the pub in the 1990s he was plagued by doors slamming, in particular one with a hydraulic arm designed to make closure a slow process – yet a force would occasionally defy the laws of physics. Colin never observed a ghost himself, but he recalled a particularly tough female regular who was seriously spooked one day and fled the pub. When she eventually had the courage to return, she described having seen the apparition of a little man with a flat cap, looking for all the world like cartoon character Andy Capp, walk through the bar and disappear into a wall. Subsequent research revealed that there had previously been a doorway there. Incidentally, Andy's creator, Reg

Smythe (1917–98), lived in Hartlepool and like his chauvinist alter ego enjoyed visiting pubs for inspiration. Cartoon strip barman Jackie was based on his old friend Jackie Maclean. When Jackie ran the Seaton Hotel, Reg could sometimes be seen sitting contemplatively alone in a corner.

But there's another ghost on the Headland sporting a flat cap. Live-in landlady's son Chris Wallace, who has resided at the Harbour of Refuge pub for three years, recalled to me being unable to sleep one night during 2013 and went downstairs at around 5 a.m., sensing something untoward. There he encountered a woman leaving the ladies' toilet and walking towards the restaurant motioning 'as if putting on a storm coat'. When mentioning this later to one of the regulars, both simultaneously glimpsed

Deceased landlady Lorna Whittingham still makes her presence felt at Hartlepool's The Ship, near the Fish Quay.
(© Paul Screeton)

the same apparition, although to Chris it was more a black shadow seen out of the corner of his eye. He then learned that both she and a former landlord, wearing his familiar flat cap 'just like Andy', but called Albert, were regularly seen and treated with familiarity. In Croft Gardens, only a few yards from the pub (which is known colloquially as 'the Pot House' in memory of its former glazed façade), stands the statue commemorating Andy Capp. How appropriate.

Another Headland boozer I visited was The Ship, trying to verify the veracity of reports of a phantom woman. Down-to-earth patrons who had been regulars for donkeys' years dismissed the report in the *Hartlepool Mail* as a total non-story. A faded cutting reported that landlord Roy Carny found that pictures constantly fell from walls, so he moved them to another room, where they hung undisturbed. Hardly 'hold the front page' stuff, but in 1993, two women reported seeing a third appear from nowhere and a similar claim was made by another regular a few months afterwards. It was supposedly the wraith of a former land-lady, named Lorna. My sleuthing got no further than ascertaining that there was a landlady from the 1950s called Lorna Whittingham.

Lastly, some pubs in the Durham hin-terland, starting with the Village Inn, Easington Village, are familiar with a woman called Emily who was knocked down outside the pub many years ago. She died after being taken into the cellar for treatment, accompanied by her dog. Landlady Gail Pallister told the author:

The spirit of Emily at the Village Inn, Easington Village, objected to swearing. (© Paul Screeton)

She's mischievous and moves things, particularly during the renovation two years ago, when workmen's tools and confectionery for breaks would vanish totally or reappear elsewhere. I'm in a paranormalist group and at a psychic demonstration was told without prompting that 'an Emily is upset by an electrician's swearing and he has to stop it'.

Gail also told me that when she owned the village's Masons Arms, her nursery-age daughter befriended one of two little girl spirits – who Gail could also see – one of whom appeared in a Victorian-era print hanging in the pub.

But Gail's psychic interface with the spirit world and pubs does not end there. As landlady of another East Durham pub, the Fir Tree in Wingate, she awoke one night to encounter five ghostly figures. Closing her eyes did not make them disappear. One told her enigmatically, 'We all come here.' Gail later learned the pub had previously acted as a mortuary before burial took place.

Meanwhile, at the Pemberton Arms, Haswell, landlord Fred Harris engaged the services of a spiritualist medium to find out about the presence he felt watching him occasionally. The ghostbuster claimed to have contacted the spirit the publican could sense, and that he had been hanged as a criminal in the Pemberton Arms during its early days during the 1860s. The miscreant had been involved in fraud and embezzlement and suffered the consequences.

FOUR

POLTERGEISTS AND MISCHIEF

POLTERGEISTS are not true ghosts. They are a very different phenomenon: the 'polt' is heard but not seen, and the ghost is seen and only occasionally heard. Ghosts rarely speak and certainly do not behave in pantomimic rising and falling wails or to the accompaniment of clanking chains. Ghost hunters who take themselves seriously find poltergeists of particular scientific interest because they do produce physical effects which can be measurable. Even the name, whose source lies in the German for noisy spirit, tells of its practicability for objective examination and it also has the advantage that such mischievous, disruptive and destructive activity can be mapped within a narrow pattern of knocking, the moving and throwing of objects, opening and closing doors, turning taps on and off, all of which smacks of a schoolboy's silly stunt rather than the Devil's demonic deception; more the naughty corner than bell, book and candle. Not warranting liturgical involvement, nor needing spiritual or secular mediumship, it's the parapsychologist's territory, where poltergeists have been classified as 'recurrent spontaneous psychokinesis' – or in the reductionist vocabulary, RSPK.

One last point, it seems de rigueur whenever commenting on poltergeist phenomena – and that even includes sceptics – to commit the sin of including some (unsubstantiated) reference to the focus being a human and mostly focussing upon a puberty-age member of the family, usually a teenage daughter. Even eminent psychologist Carl Gustav Jung believed individual humans were responsible and he called it a 'catalytic exteriorisation phenomenon'. So, let's investigate some regional examples from my files.

Where better to start than the oldest district of Hartlepool: Stranton, and its attractive Blacksmith's Arms. A busy modern dual-carriageway carries traffic past this pub, which is almost the oldest hostelry in town. It certainly still looks like a typical village inn from the outside, despite much restoration. The steep gables suggest seventeenth-century construction and in the wall overlooking All Saints churchyard can be seen a single tiny window. Here the publican was charged with keeping a vigilant eye after funerals at the beginning of the nineteenth century, when body-snatching was a lucrative if gruesome profession of ne'er do wells. As for any ghostlore, it has had at least two claimants on its haunted reputation. One resident claimed she and her father heard the doorbell ringing during the night shortly after her mother's death, but the doorbell had been dismantled weeks before the spectral sound. Then there is 'George', championed as a mischievous poltergeist struggling to be released from his earthly bondage. Whatever the presence was, pub regulars had ticked off the familiar poltergeist phenomena list: the temperature suddenly dropping, doors and windows mysteriously opening and shutting, glasses being moved and bottles falling off the optics. Both current landlord David Mountney and his opposite number mere yards away in the Brewery Tap, Marie-Louise McKay, agree that little spooky activity currently happens in the Blacksmith's. However, there was once a really censorious licensee at the 'White House' (as it was best known, for its colour) and when Marie-Louise was slightly underage to be drinking, but one of the taller teenagers in a group of five 'lasses on the lash' of a Friday night, she and a friend would enter ahead of three friends who were 6 inches shorter. But the vertically challenged trio would feel as if they had hit an invisible barrier.

One of Hartlepool's oldest and most haunted inns, The Blacksmith's Arms. (© Paul Screeton)

Maybe a rationalist would suggest their consciences were at work, but the girls attributed the force to the supernatural presence of the ex-landlord, who was also an ex-policeman and father, still enforcing his legal right to bar entry to transgressors. A medium identified the threshold guardian as 'George' and Marie-Louise's subsequent research for her book on Hartlepool pub history, *The Lion Roars and the Monkey Bites*, found two possible contenders called George who had been host.

Another ancient Stranton pub, called The Stranton until recently, dates from the 1730s. Today it doubles as a drinking establishment and visitor centre known as the Brewery Tap. It began life as the Anchor, when Hartlepool Bay almost came to its front door. Mischief is occasionally afoot in the building and brewery guide/landlady Marie-Louise McKay personally witnessed an extraordinary display of the paranormal. 'This was the weirdest thing I have ever seen in here,'

The 'bodysnatchers' window' of the Blacksmith's Arms, overlooking All Saints' cemetery. (© Paul Screeton)

Marie-Louise told me. 'I was on my own in the bar one Sunday when I watched three photo albums rise up – levitating! Then they shot across the room at lightning speed and banged against the wall. I'm a sceptic about such things, but I saw it myself. It certainly couldn't have been a draught.' She also related mischief in the upstairs kitchen where washing-up is done after visitors leave. Frequently the sink plug will disappear, only to reappear several days later. Similarly a gold watch went AWOL for two weeks. On a more personal and paraphysical level, the spirit in the cellar has been tentatively identified by a medium as a very tall former landlord who would bump his head on the low ceiling. There have been reports of the wraith stooping, banging into kegs as if they were in his way and whistling to himself.

Another pub with a fascinating history of the paranormal is the Half Moon in Easington Village. Facing across the village green, the inn has seen more than 300 years of history pass through its doors. It also has the unenviable reputation of attracting persons with an unhappy personal history – particularly those whose marriages were somewhat rocky. The resident ghost, known to regulars as 'Robert', is a restless soul with a long pedigree reaching back to the days when the pub functioned as a coaching inn. Back in the nineteenth century, the Half Moon employed a particularly pretty barmaid with whom Robert, a patron who was a humble road sweeper, was besotted. At every opportunity Robert would be in the hostelry mooning over the serving wench, but his affections were not reciprocated; instead she married a rich suitor. Heartbroken, Robert went to the inn's stables and

Surrounded by Camerons Brewery, the Brewery Tap lays claim to having Stranton's oldest pub foundation, although the present building is likely to be nineteenth century and the façade considerably modernised. (© Paul Screeton)

hanged himself. Now, a century and a half later, Robert still hangs around, unable to leave the scene of his unrequited love and suicide. It is believed that the stables were incorporated when the Half Moon was modernised at some stage. Bringing the pub up to modern standards did nothing to deter Robert's residency and his presence continued to wax and wane, even following the turning year with seasonal activity. Spooky behaviour would start around November and continue until Christmas had passed, only for mysterious goings-on to resume in the spring, always in April.

Seasoned spectre sleuth Margaret O'Rourke, of the *Hartlepool Mail*, was able to piece together a portrait of the haunting from widowed landlady Mary Bracchi in the 1970s. She revealed:

He doesn't frighten me. Robert is not evil in the sense that some hauntings make you feel frightened. I've lived with him for around fourteen years, yet I know that temporary managers who have come here to take over during my holidays have refused to look after the pub ever again. I'd say that Robert is an unhappy man and that he cannot bear happiness around him. That's why in the past our staff has mainly been made up of barmaids who were either in the throes of divorce or who had just put an unhappy marriage behind them. I'd say unhappiness follows this place as no one is allowed to be happy here. Perhaps Robert in his own unhappiness reaches out from the past to the unhappy folk of the world.

Mary's husband was still alive when they took over the Half Moon and, although a sceptic, he came to believe the pub was haunted. Shortly after his death, an aunt was visiting and after being told the footsteps she heard during the night were not made by any human as no one was out of bed, she declined to ever return. Some of Robert's antics were more in the nature of poltergeist behaviour. The chef, two barmaids and Mary's daughter witnessed a heavy plastic container containing concentrated washing-up liquid fly through the air and narrowly miss seriously injuring one of those barmaids. A beer tap was seen to turn itself on of its own volition; beer barrels were heard moving noisily in the cellar when Mary was alone in bed; letters from her daughter swished from her hands as if by a gale-force wind and the heavy springs of the entrance door clicked as if a customer had entered, yet no one approached the counter. Keys would also vanish and just as mysteriously return

Another coaching inn, dating back to 1635, is Trimdon's Red Lion which was in the news for yet another Grey Lady haunting. Friendly and full of mischief, this ghostly female was habitually interfering with gas taps and the cellar's cooling system. Ted Parker, who was landlord in 1992, reported that 'one of the draymen had a brush with her a few weeks ago. He heard the hissing of gas and adjusted one of the gas taps to put it right. By the time he had finished in the cellar the tap had been moved and was letting out air again.'

Yet another *Hartlepool Mail* journalist with an interest in the paranormal was Bernice Saltzer. She described a house in Dalkeith Road, Hartlepool, as 'what easily could be dubbed the most haunted in Hartlepool'. The article was illustrated with a double-exposure photograph of the resident, crockery and radiator. This anonymous semi-detached is where crockery was thrown about and

Landlady Marie-Louise McKay watched books levitate and shoot across the bar at the Brewery Tap. (© Paul Screeton)

Easington Village's *Half Moon* inn experiences poltergeist behaviour from an invisible thwarted suitor named Robert. (© Paul Screeton)

the central-heating battled an unmistakable chilliness. No-nonsense resident Jean McLean, who had lived in her home for more than thirty years, maintained that there was a poltergeist. She and her husband had seen cups and saucers flying off the dresser, the gas fire being turned on and off, drops in temperature and many occurrences of footsteps being heard. If poltergeist phenomena are associated with youngsters passing through puberty, she fit the bill as a mother of nine children. However, a man with far, far more experience of the paranormal than I, David Taylor, founder of parapsychology research group Parasearch, tells me that statistically this theory fails to stand up. Anyway, there seem to have been multiple presences causing mayhem at this house and every one of her children and her second husband had seen or heard something uncanny. Jean said:

Things first started not long after we moved in and two of my daughters saw a man in a trilby hat and a mac in their bedroom. I thought it must have been their father, my first husband. My husband has seen my first husband in the back bedroom and he won't go in there. We've seen an old woman and there'd been a smell of roses which someone at the spiritualist church told me was my mother. My son-in-law won't stay here anymore because he slept on the settee one night and he saw a woman standing in the corner.

She believed the ghosts were family members – except for sightings of a spectral cat. Also Jean's description of 'two of the children said that one night they felt like something heavy was pressing down on them and they couldn't move' fits almost perfectly the classic 'old hag' experience

Trimdon Village's Red Lion has a classic Grey Lady in residence. (© Paul Screeton)

explored by folklorist David J. Hufford in his groundbreaking book *The Terror That Comes in the Night*. The only problem is that Hufford was writing about sleep paralysis, rare enough normally, but for two people to experience it concurrently stretches the theory to the limit and some other explanation must be looked for, however unpalatable to sceptics of the supernatural realm. Neither was it traditional poltergeist behaviour, but at least the family remained stoical about sharing their home with uncalled-for guests.

Staying in Hartlepool, just down the road from where I came into this world at Grantully Nursing Home, and a reminder of the pre-nationalisation South Durham Steel and Iron Company, is the South Durham Social Club in Westbourne Road. For reasons best known to themselves, the governing committee wanted no publicity about one

of their regulars. Like a red rag to a bull, the *Hartlepool Mail*'s Margaret O'Rourke defied the club's bureaucracy and wrote about the temperamental nuisance who crashed doors shut, smashed glasses and during alterations threw a workman's saw across the concert room. 'Charlie', as he was not too affectionately known, had a favourite haunt in the upstairs billiards room, but would also wander his shabbily dressed way along the downstairs corridors. Living members would find the old gentleman staring silently at them. But it's hard to bar a fiery red-headed Irish journalist from reporting the goings-on of a newsworthy contact with the otherworld.

Sadly, just as pubs are in decline, so is the club trade and Greatham Social Club was one of the earliest in the area to call 'time'. Four villages on the periphery are regarded as satellites of Hartlepool and indeed the tentacles of housing from the self-governing unitary authority have almost reached all of them. Greatham, the southernmost, lies on a ridge where Bishop Robert Sitchill founded an alms hospital and endowed it with the entire Greatham manor. Unsurprisingly, that archetypal figure the Grey Lady haunts the pretty environs, although her appearances seem to have waned dramatically over the past several decades. Perhaps it was sheer desperation or lack of originality to lay the blame for inexplicable footsteps, banging sounds and unknown voices during 1968 at Greatham Social Club on her ladyship – even inexplicable toilet flushings. During the late 1960s I picked up a tale that Greatham Social Club was haunted. The sound of a toilet being flushed could be heard, but when investigated there was no human present. The ablutions were blamed on the resident spook. I rang whoever was the

A Grey Lady was blamed for various anomalous happenings – including flushing a toilet – at Greatham Social Club. Even she could not forestall its closure. (John Pollard, photo courtesy of Hartlepool Mail)

Poltergeist Charlie is still active at Hartlepool's South Durham Social Club. (© Paul Screeton)

club steward at the time to check out the veracity of the rumour. From memory, I can recall neither affirmation or denial but his words of wisdom to me: 'It's not the dead you have to worry about son, it's the living.' The story was spiked in the end, no doubt depriving the financially struggling club of publicity.

Now we move on to the notorious Crying Boy pictures, many variations of which exist. According to contemporary legend, they encourage bad luck and during house blazes are nigh on indestructible. Reporter Paul Wenham mentioned both strands in his *Hartlepool Mail* report on a house in Hartlepool's Cornwall Street. Essentially, these mass-produced portraits of tearful boys – and girls – by artist Bruno Amadio, an Italian also known as Giovanni Bragolin, were widely distributed from the 1950s onwards. In 1985 a report in *The Sun* had a firefighter from Yorkshire claiming that undamaged copies of the painting were frequently found amidst the ruins of burned houses. Having stated that no firefighter would allow a copy of the painting into his own house, tabloid newspapers ran numerous reports on house fires suffered by people who had owned one of the paintings. Editor of *The Sun*, Kelvin MacKenzie, seized upon the notion of a supposed curse and had his paper organise a mass bonfire of the paintings sent in by readers. Apparently the best way to lift the curse, it is said, is to give the painting to another person or reunite the boy and girl and hang them together. As for their flameproof resistance quality, my friend David Clarke, an award-winning journalism lecturer in Sheffield, demythologised this phenomenon after having discovered they are made of a heat-resistant material. Picking

up on Dr Clarke's original research, writer and comedian Steve Punt investigated the curse of the crying boy in the BBC Radio Four production *Punt PI*. Following testing at the Building Research Establishment, it was found that the prints were treated with a fire-repellant-containing varnish and the string the painting was hung on would be the first to burn, resulting in the painting landing face down on the floor and thus being protected. End of curse, end of story.

The human element in this particular story was resident Christine Fothergill, who, when a picture fell from the wall, found it 'yielded an eerie secret' – two Crying Boy prints behind the frame. Four other pictures produced more of the same behind the frames: a mystery in itself. Christine then listed a catalogue of family 'calamities': boiler explosion, broken washing machine, bust video recorder, car broken into twice and husband Stephen hit by a flying sheet of metal. We all have periods when nothing seems to go right and Christine conceded: 'I'm not really superstitious. These things could have happened if the prints hadn't been behind the pictures.'

Being a long-time resident of Seaton Carew, The Schooner is one of the author's occasional watering holes and unusually for a modern pub (built 1993) has an old-fashioned ghost. It was built to the design of founding owner Harold 'H' Hugill and was named The Schooner after H's architect remarked that the drawing reminded him of a schooner.

Staff had been plagued by minor mischievousness and seen vague shapes, but an unnamed waitress reported the form of a pipe-smoking man dressed in tweeds from around the 1930s–40s. I became involved when I heard the large, long

Tricks have been played by an unseen presence that staff members have named George at Seaton Carew's Schooner estate pub. (© Paul Screeton)

mirror fixed to the wall in the ladies' loo had been found one morning smashed to smithereens, even though the facility had been checked after the pub closed. A family-oriented new estate pub, since its opening a friendly, playful spirit named George had played tricks. Bar manager Brian Wiley's mongrel Rusty, which had never behaved strangely at other pubs he had managed, had howled as if sensing an unseen presence. His wife, Ali, reported objects moving when no one was touching them in the bar and their flat, where the computer would also turn itself on an off. Additionally, objects would fall from the shelves in the kitchen. Even I noticed sturdy menus falling over on adjacent table number 33 for two days running in 1999, sufficient for me to make a note of the occurrences. As for the mirror which had remained attached to the wall, maybe George shattered it as he did not like his ghostly reflection.

What might have given a teen/polt connection is an ancient seafront pub in Seaton Carew, the Seaton Hotel. Dating back to the eighteenth century, it was built on the former site of the Ship Inn as a coaching house with six adjoining lodging houses to cater for the wealthy Quaker visitors who made the resort popular. The name given to the hotel was the New Inn, which was eventually changed to Seaton Hotel. When owned in the late twentieth century by engineer Kevin Jones and his wife Denise, a hospital path lab technician, their 14-year-old son Anthony complained of eerie knockings coming from the long-abandoned attic above the room where he slept. But this can't be dismissed as hormonal energies being discharged, because while he was staying away his mother slept in his room and was terrified by the same tappings during the night. The knocking only occurred

Seaton Carew's oldest and most haunted hostelry is the Seaton Hotel. (© Paul Screeton)

after dark and Kevin told the *Hartlepool Mail*'s Margaret O'Rourke: 'There are no pipes in the room or on the outside wall. It's just knocking that starts and stops. There's no rational explanation.' Seaton Hotel's long history dates back to when wreckers operated from Seaton Carew, hoping to lure ships on to the treacherous Longscar Rocks in Hartlepool Bay and salvage the rich pickings from the cargoes. Loss of life was of no concern to them, and when the bodies reached the shore they were taken to a room set aside for the purpose in the hotel, washed and prepared for burial in the nearby graveyard of Holy Trinity church. Kevin Jones mused to the reporter: 'With that kind of history it makes you wonder.'

Wonder indeed! Local historian Maureen Anderson, a regular who collected a number of ghost tales for her book *Tales, Trials & Treasure of Seaton Carew*, was told of a legend that in the Ship Inn's day a coachman's wife was murdered on the premises. Maureen pondered the possibility of her being the root cause of the haunting. and wrote:

The common description is a female with hair styled in braids on top of her head and the impression of a long flowing plain dress, although no one has actually seen her below the waist. She has often been 'felt', a light touch on the leg, blankets being pulled down when someone has been in bed, a touch on the shoulder. One room in the hotel, which many years ago was numbered 19 until decorating took place and the numbers were removed from the doors, was always very cold and people who slept there and had never heard of the ghost, said the room had an eerie chill to it.

Reopening under new ownership at Christmas 2012 reactivated a return of the uncanny, and new landlord Darren Juler told me how he and others would be wafted by the smell of a women's perm conditioner, one particular door would open and shut of its own volition and a spectre appeared and disappeared in the seat nearest to it. Far from being phased by the experience, Darren had previously been host of a pub in Ferryhill, County Durham, which was featured in the popular *Most Haunted* TV programme.

Finally, actress Janice Margaret Graveson, who was born in Easington, lived mainly in Peterlee, studied at Durham University and moved to London. Along the way she claims to have acquired a playful poltergeist. Probably best known as Jan Graveson for her role as pregnant runaway Disa O'Brien in *EastEnders*, she recalled: 'It used to amuse itself by playing practical jokes on me. I know most people would probably be afraid of a ghost, but I thought it was fun having it around.' It followed her to Durham University and kept her company as she studied:

> It used to petrify my friends when it began playing all its juvenile pranks, but I would just tell them not to worry. It would get all of my mobiles spinning at once and I would just lie back in bed and watch the show in awe. I sometimes felt like the privileged guest at a one-man show.

Eventually, Jan's mother ordered her to get rid of the ghost. 'I told it to go away

Easington-born actress Jan Graveson acquired her own playful poltergeist. (Author's collection)

and it obeyed, but sometimes I still feel a presence,' said Jan, who can still be seen regularly on television and in films.

Jan Graveson may have enacted the role of a troubled teenager on TV and personally encouraged poltergeist behaviour, but that hardly constitutes the preferred scapegoat approach for such manifestations. The examples from my files suggest some instances of person-focussed cases, but no significant teenage correlation. Perhaps these low-key events are the rule rather than the exception, as in classic cases such as Enfield, Pontefract and South Shields.

Poltergeists may be traditionally noisy, but these ones amuse rather than scare. Why? Well, the North East is generally acknowledged as the friendliest region in the UK, so why should our spirits be any different?

FIVE

HISTORICAL HAUNTINGS (EAST DURHAM)

A former vicar of the church of St Thomas á Becket, Grindon, told a newspaper interviewer in 1972 about the apparitions associated with this neglected church. Since then the ruins have fascinated me, but the ghosts have remained elusive. When Thorpe Thewles expanded more than a century ago and the population shifted – not to mention the already parlous state of the building, begun in 1131 – it was decided to close the church and build a new one in the centre of the new settlement. Parts were transferred to the new place of worship, including an altar top of black Cleveland marble and the stone font. Designated a Grade 'A' ancient monument, when I was last there it had warnings not to approach too closely due to its crumbling state. More controversially, there is a tale that when the church was abandoned villagers left behind the very flagstone on which it is believed Thomas á Becket was murdered in 1170. Perhaps this is as fanciful as the supposed reason for his death: that four villainous knights thought they were doing their monarch a favour by murdering the Archbishop of Canterbury, after King Henry II was heard to utter, 'Who will rid me of this turbulent priest?' The musing was just that – exasperation at his former best friend whom he had made head of the Church to whip its clerics into line with the State, but who had 'gone native'. The words had been meant rhetorically if, in fact, these were his words at all, as there is no evidence to back up the claim. Despite this, on 29 December, Becket's skull was sliced in two and his brains smeared on the cold stone floor. It is said that witnesses rushed to soak their shirts in his blood, one of whom supposedly took the bloodied garment home to his paralysed wife, who requested he mix it with water and bathe her with it. Hers was one of 400 miracles attributed to Thomas and it took little more than two years before the Pope authorised his canonisation. Thomas's Canterbury tomb became the fourth most popular shrine in Christendom, ranking only after Rome, Jerusalem and Santiago de Compostela.

Maybe Grindon is worthy of pilgrimage or a spot of ghosthunting. Is Thomas himself one of the apparitions said to haunt the ruined church?

But Grindon is not the only abandoned hamlet in the area, for at Embleton it is said the ghosts of former villagers return annually to drink in the local inn, worship at the church and dance on the village green. It is also said that on certain days the bell in the former school can be heard ringing.

A more modern spectre haunts Thorpe Thewles railway station. Following the Railway Mania of the nineteenth century, the main east-coast route from London King's Cross to Edinburgh passed through Wynyard and Thorpe Thewles, before a more direct challenge from a line via Darlington and Durham City gained precedence. The railway here was abandoned half a century ago, but a section of it forms a pleasant walkway and takes in Wynyard Country Park. During the line's heyday in the First World War, the Thorpe Thewles stationmaster was murdered and his body found by his opposite number down the line at Wynyard, Mr G. Dodds. A group of Russian immigrant refugees working in the nearby woods and camped in the vicinity were the prime suspects, but nothing was ever proved. Since then, numerous sightings of his ghostly form have been reported. Also, in recent years, so too have visitations by a small ghost girl.

A road leads directly from here in a south-west direction to Norton-on-Tees. It is Blakeston (or Blakiston) Lane and just off it was a quarry where, in 1877, a fox led a dozen hounds of the South Durham and Cleveland Hunt to their deaths over a 160-foot drop. As if to warn of the nearby danger, a phantom dog first began appearing the vicinity in 1892. More recently, five witnesses in a vehicle thought they had hit it in 1982.

As for picturesque Norton itself, the orchard at the back of the Red Lion was the scene of a duel in 1806. At a soiree, an argument developed between a

The crumbling ruins of Grindon's church of St Thomas à Becket, photographed in 1987. (© Paul Screeton)

Trains may be in Thorpe Thewles' past, but a former stationmaster and small girl haunt the Wynyard Forest visitor centre's vicinity to this day. (© Paul Screeton)

Captain Stapleton, a regular army officer who had been serving in the Peninsular War, and a Coronet Gray, a militiaman. Stapleton implied that the other's fancy uniform and not being posted abroad had given the militiaman an advantage in wooing the girls. Gray took this as a slur and in the duel which followed was fatally wounded. Stapleton kept the facts quiet as his commander, the Duke of Wellington, forbade duelling, and the officer was eventually killed in France. Gray continued to haunt the spot and it is said that twice during 1987 the sounds of double pistol shots were heard, even waking people up.

Boundary changes have moved Wynyard Estate from Durham into north-west Cleveland, but paranormal activity knows no such artificial barriers

and the ubiquitous Grey Lady ignores arbitrary administrative demarcation lines drawn on a local government map. Sightings find her initially travelling down Gas House Road and finally emerging from large mirrors in the Duke's Gallery inside Wynyard Hall. This splendid mansion was the most magnificent in County Durham, being built for the 3rd Marquess of Londonderry, whose fortune rested upon the county's rich coal seams and the exportation of the 'black gold' via Seaham Harbour, a port he created to avoid the cost of shipping it via the Wear or Tyne. The stately home was later bought by a magnate of a different hue, appropriately a former mining surveyor, Sir John Hall, mastermind of Gateshead's MetroCentre, Europe's largest indoor shopping mall.

On one notable occasion decades ago, the burglar alarm went off and arriving guests, accompanied by gamekeeper George Douglas, made a fruitless search for intruders. They heard doors slamming mysteriously, but all they found was that they were locked out of their rooms. The Grey Lady was blamed for both denying guests entry and also bolting them in. The mischievous spirit was said to make a nocturnal journey to the hall each night and on one occasion, having secured the party's firearms in the gunroom after a day's shooting, Ray Hawkey was walking his two dogs towards Lion Bridge when the animals became spooked, held back and began barking. The estate worker became terrified when he witnessed a woman heading towards him, dressed in a cloak and bonnet. She seemed to float past him, her body a yard or so off the ground. Also the Lion Bridge entrance to the 2,500-acre (or 6,500 in another account) estate has its resident wraith, a maid who supposedly threw herself off the bridge and into the water below during the late nineteenth century. Her activity has been attributed to annoyance at being disturbed in her watery abode in 1963, when the lake was dredged. Some accounts fuse the two spirits into a single Grey Lady, who drowned in the lake and was angered by major developments under Cameron Hall ownership. Certainly the burgeoning business park development has made the place very busy and any self-respecting spectre would be alarmed to find her old haunts are the domain of exclusive housing for millionaire footballers and entrepreneurs.

The splendid nineteenth-century mansion Wynyard Hall was built for the 3rd Marquess of Londonderry. (© Paul Screeton)

It is rare for a ghost story to have a humorous aspect. Particularly in this case, as the apparition has previosuly been described as 'horrendous' for no specified reason. It apparently haunted the former rectory in the scenic country town of Sedgefield – famed for its Shrove Tuesday ball game – throughout most of the eighteenth century. The apparition was known locally as the Pickled Parson and for good reason. At the time, the rector of Sedgefield was one of the wealthiest clergymen in the Bishopric of Durham. The lucrative stipend involved collecting tithes for his and the parish church's income. The church land was hired to farmers in the form of rents, which were payable each 20 December. Therefore it was unfortunate that the rector died a week before the rents were due. Not one to let a minor mishap such as her husband's death interfere with the financial imperative of tax collection, his wily widow resourcefully placed his corpse in an empty room, salted the body to preserve it and kept it hidden there (or in another version, propped it up in a window for all to see) until all the rents had been collected. She then announced his passing. But that was not closure; rather the parson seemed to want retribution for having been treated in such a disrespectful manner upon death. He retained an earthly presence, albeit as a disgruntled spectre, scaring all and sundry in the parish to which his spirit was earthbound (or at least until the long-suffering villagers got relief when the rectory burned down towards the end of the century). Having been demolished after the blaze, the same year a new rectory was built in 1793 for

Multiple tales involving Lion Bridge make this a particularly spooky spot on the Wynyard Estate. (© Paul Screeton)

a landed gentleman who took over the post and it was erected to match the style of living to which he was accustomed. When its predecessor was built, thankfully for local residents the ghost failed to manifest again. Converted in 1973 to a community association building for general use and named Ceddesfield Hall, it is rumoured the ghost of the Pickled Parson still dwells within a secret passage between the former rectory and St Edmund's church, perhaps also appearing above ground.

Moving to the coast, no book claiming to be at least a partial record of haunting in East Durham could fail to recognise the contribution to the study made by the late Reginald Wright. Born in 1913, the son of a pitman in Dawdon, he became a self-published historian, poet, folklorist and composer, although after investing £700 into the 1986 festive recording of 'Merry Christmas Queen Mother', with the aid of 1,500 Hartlepool schoolchildren, it did not sell a single copy, even to the families of those performing! His written contributions to local lore were a bizarre scattergun of reminiscences and snippets of half-remembered narrative folklore. But they cannot be ignored as they contain gems of value. It has to be conceded that Reg knew his patch well and shared his findings with enthusiasm. He certainly helped me when I was researching a special colour supplement for the *Hartlepool Mail*. In Reg's *A History of Castle Eden Lore in Search of King Arthur*, he writes: 'The village's ghostlore says phantoms haunt every step you take, where pieces of thong (talismans) or chain can still be found hanging on trees and bushes, but they simply vanish into thin air when touched.' He referred to the place as the 'Village of Perception'.

There is nothing wrong with wild speculation, but don't always expect it to be believed. Reg's portrait of King Arthur and his henchmen having a close association with Castle Eden and Blackhall is no more ludicrous than the depiction of the Once and Future King, chivalrous knights in chain mail and magnificent mediaeval castle, as in the film *Camelot*. There is absolutely no historical substance to this Hollywood revisionism, but Reg persists and introduces the notion of there being a true castle, a Geordie Camelot that could be seen 'rising in a mist above the modern housing of Peterlee New Town every Midsummer's Eve – only to vanish before it can be pointed out by the observer'. As was recorded in 1542: 'Sum tyme the people see a fomose toun of castle.' The nearest to documentary proof for all this Arthuriana speculation is an 1801 map of the district with the name 'Kamlan' where Crimdon now exists with its caravan park, dene and memories of it as the 'Pitmen's Riviera'. It is also known for a beauty pageant, which local MP Emanuel Shinwell played truant from his duties as armaments minister to be a judge of during the last war and for which he was lampooned by the headline: 'Shinwell puts legs before arms'. Reg claimed the letter 'K' did not exist in the Anglo-Saxon language, so it should have been spelled 'Camlan'. Arthur reportedly fought twelve battles, the last being known as Camlan and ploughing a field above the dene revealed many skeletons of men and boys as if pitched into a mass grave. But we can all play this name game. What of the Catcote district of Hartlepool, where a Romano-British settlement was excavated in the 1960s: why not have this as the site of the Arthurian battle Cat Coit Celidon?

The knights of the fabled Round Table, according to Reg, appeared during daylight hours disguised as a clutch of chickens at a T-junction in Castle Eden village. As for Blackhall, the cliffs above the beach are pitted with caves, one of which is known as Arthur's Cave and in his *History, Topography, and Directory of the County Palatine of Durham*, Francis Whellan recorded:

> At Hesleden Dene in June 1894, an aperture was discovered on the side of the hill which proved to be the entrance to a large cave. On further search being made, human skeletons were found, one of which was a very large size. These when discovered seemed nearly perfect, but on being brought to light, they crumbled away. History and tradition are alike silent relative to this cave. The cave was gloomy and unfathomable.

England's defender's name is also attached to an earthwork, Arthur's Tor, opposite the T-junction where the road from Hutton Henry meets the A19, traditionally hollow and containing treasure guarded by giant soldiers and haunted by a knight in golden armour. According to Reg, a cairn on its summit was excavated in 1932 and a man's skeleton with a military breastplate was exhumed. The A19 sweeps towards Sheraton through what Reg says was known in olden times as the 'Valley of the Graves'. Sheraton was where another fictional 'royal' lived, eponymous TV series hero Jason King, aka Peter Wyngarde. Reg also introduced the prime legend that Arthur himself is laid asleep slumbering with his court surrounding him, awaiting the call to arms to save his country from whatever

foe in times of peril. In the book account, there's a vault where the lost castle stood and a peasant found it and woke Arthur, but because he did not blow a horn the king just went back to sleep.

Another maverick but more erudite writer, S.G. Wildman, proposed a novel theory in his 1971 book *The Black Horsemen*: that Black Horse pub names symbolised the fifth-century cavalry of King Arthur and his cohorts. Sam argued that this sturdy form of rugged black pony provided a rapid response force and that the White Horse names signified the invading Saxons and their lighter steeds. So might there be here a connection with Reg's claim that hundreds of riderless horses were twice seen cantering through Wellfield in 1835? More vanishing horses were recorded on 22 July 1892 at Wheatley Hill in broad daylight. Reg believed them to be visions from mediaeval times, with the explanation that it was typical of horses fleeing a battlefield after their riders had been slain. There is even a highly descriptive account of the last encounter by a John Wilson:

> We stood some considerable time and I couldn't help but notice the white foaming sweat standing on the glistening black skins of these magnificent animals trotting forty to fifty neck-and-neck. It was wholly unexpected, an extraordinary sight, and my father who stood beside me made the sign of the Cross, but in less than two or three minutes (it seemed) they all vanished – not one of them was to be seen. The day was close and sultry, we could hardly breathe. I will never doubt that I saw them as long as I live. I am not an intemperate fellow.

So, just how trustworthy are ghost tales of yore? Reg admitted in another of his books, *Black Hall Rocks and Blackhall*, that this had 'hitherto not been recorded in anyone's records or remembered by most people except one very old gentleman who had the information given to him by his father'. So at least its antiquity, if singular provenance, is guaranteed. The tale concerns a pub called the Pig and Whistle, whose name derivation has been suggested as an adaptation from the Saxon 'Piggen' (a milking pail) and 'Wassail' (to be in good health). Also beer was originally served in pails carried amongst patrons by the publican owner into which customers dipped their mugs, which were called 'Pigs'. There are several other rival origins claimed, such as a salutation to the Virgin Mary or a free translation of 'going to pot'. But I digress. Apparently the pub was a sturdy structure with walls at least 4-feet thick, filthy windows with wooden shutters both inside and outside, plus a rat-infested thatched roof. It was said that the owner's wife was induced by her lover to murder her husband. As instructed, she sliced up his corpse and, rather appropriately for the inn's name, fed his carcass pieces to her swine. But there was not to be a happy ending, for the sacrificial victim of the couple's lust haunted the illicit lovers to the extent that they felt forced to confess their complicity to the authorities. In those days the legal process ran more swiftly than today and the lothario was hanged, drawn and quartered on a gibbet erected on the coastal cliffs close to Dead Man's Bank, at the foot of which was the pub where the deed was committed. The landlady suffered an equally gruesome fate, supposedly buried alive at Castle Eden. According to legend,

the twenty-first-century observer may sit on a dark night near the site of the former pub and enjoy the eerie sound of revellers carousing and maybe even espy the ghosts of smugglers bringing their booty ashore.

Also in the vicinity, an aged recluse chose to live in the caves of Blackhall Rocks, but one day fell asleep under a haystack on the land of a farmer name Chrystal. Unfortunately, a farmworker innocently but fatally pierced him with a pitchfork. After the accident it was discovered that the unfortunate man had around £2,000 in his pockets. According to Reg Wright his ghost is said to still frequent the area; looking for his life's savings, perhaps.

Also in Blackhall Rocks lies an imposing building which today acts as a high-class hotel and restaurant, trading as Hardwicke Hall Manor so as to avoid confusion with the similarly named Hardwick Hall, in Sedgefield. It became a Roman Catholic centre from around 1590 and from 1600 until 1824 had a Jesuit chaplain. I have had the privilege of a guided tour and visited the priest's hide in one of its garrets. The hide was probably constructed by Father Richard Holtby, who was an excellent carpenter and mason. Though only an amateur, it is said that no pursuivant ever discovered a hide of his manufacture. A gruesome tale from these times holds that a party of Cromwellian soldiers hunting down Roman Catholics arrived one day. But forewarned, the family had hidden their valuables and fled to safety, leaving behind only an old retainer. They reasoned that the Roundheads would not harm an elderly housekeeper, but being so incensed at finding nothing of value

Another Grey Lady spectre haunts Hardwicke Hall Manor. (Photo courtesy of Hartlepool Mail)

the soldiers tortured the old woman and, upon failing to break her will, murdered her. She is said to haunt the bridle path between Hardwicke Hall and Monk Hesleden church.

Another Hardwicke Hall story related to sectarianism has elements of both ancient and modern. When renovation work began in the early 1970s after a decade of neglect, workmen became aware of a Grey Lady who they claimed descended the staircase in a floating motion. But she was more than a mere wraith and left what some regarded as proof for a degree of physicality when three small footprints of bare feet were observed in the dry varnish after tradesmen returned the following morning. This was despite the building having been robustly secured overnight against intruders. They came from the direction of the front room, which remained locked, and disappeared into a wall.

It was as if someone had trodden in the dust in the front room and then left it imprinted into the previous day's varnishing endeavours. There seemed to be no rational explanation. But – just perhaps – there may be a tenuous connection. The mansion's resident family, the Maires, were staunch Roman Catholics at a time when their faith was unpopular. When a mob chanting 'No Popery' besieged the building, Francis Maire's wife, Ann Clavering, fled and during her hasty flight she lost her shoes. Could these mysterious prints back at the hall have recorded the passage of her tiny size 3 feet in 1972, two centuries after her death?

Yet another Grey Lady haunts former manor house, Shotton Hall, built around 1780, which became the headquarters for Peterlee Development Corporation and latterly Peterlee Town Council. When the development corporation was being wound up there was talk of whether to include the ghost in the transfer document. In typical Sunday tabloid hyperbole, she had supposedly been 'terrifying staff' for twenty years and was 'causing nightmares for lawyers' at the time of sale. A more sober assessment was given by the authority's press officer Leslie Cole. He did not believe anyone had actually seen the ghost, but only heard strange noises, including himself, who heard what sounded like a heavy file of papers dropped onto a table in the boardroom, then the focus of the haunting. When a brochure was issued by the new incumbents in the hopes of attracting tourists to visit the former stately home, it identified the Grey Lady as Gertie, a kitchen maid who committed suicide after an 'indiscretion' with one of the masters. She supposedly was last heard frequenting the stair

area which led to the former servants' quarters – where she had hanged herself. The brochure described her spirit as 'an enveloping friendly presence' who would leave the aroma of freshly baked pies, even though there was no oven at the hall. She had also been known to ring the doorbell, despite the building no longer having one.

Another Sunday tabloid story described the White House Community Centre, Eden Lane, Peterlee, as a 'rambling mansion haunted by a drunken woman ghost', whereas the local newspaper struck up the familiar tune of the Grey Lady when reporting a charity vigil. The headquarters of the Peterlee Community Association, built for a mine owner at the beginning of the twentieth century. It was also where several people claimed to have seen the ghost walking the passageways, bottle in hand, swigging merrily.

Shotton Hall prospers as a hotel today and has a friendly ghost called Gertie. (© Paul Screeton)

As for the plucky fundraisers, on a Friday the 13th 15-year-old David Price, Keith Slater and Kevin Hoyland, pupils at Howletch Comprehensive School, were locked in between 10 p.m. and 8 a.m., with the doors sealed to ensure the boys were alone. When released, Keith reported that around 1.15 a.m. they were about to try to sleep when a table fell over and hit Kevin on the head: 'I was really frightened and to calm us down we said the Lord's Prayer. As soon as we said it, the lid on the teapot flew across the room and fell on the floor. The strange thing was the milk bottle fell on the floor but there was no milk spilt. The floor stayed dry.' Keith added: 'We were worried all night and didn't dare get any sleep in case anything happened to us. At one time I also started having illusions [sic] and though it's hard to explain, we knew we were not alone.' Centre spokeswoman Brenda McWilliams commented that three weeks previous to the vigil – which raised almost £100 for a Tyneside heart research charity – workers claimed to have heard the presence sobbing.

A weird tale by reporter Steve Hilton in *The Northern Echo* involved 'legend tripping', with local people going out in all weathers and one resident dragging his wife out in just a nightie, dressing gown and slippers while others turned up in cars and minibuses. To see what? Wingate Holy Trinity's churchyard was the focus, with a gravestone which glowed. The puzzling attraction was a black marble memorial to Corporal George Henry Longstaff, of the 18th Hussars, who was killed in action in 1918. Many were claiming it was a miracle while more mundane explanations were that it was either a new securing light (the one pinpointed had actually been installed for three years) or recently installed street lamps (too far distant). The vicar, the Reverend Martin Vaizey, insisted it was not a miracle, believing it to be reflected light and 'if it was unexplained we could make money selling holy water to tourists'. National newspapers had a field day and the *Daily Mail*'s Chris Brooke elicited the fascinating adjunct from a villager: 'It's been said that if you dance twelve times around the rotten old elm tree near the church, you will be visited by the Devil. But I doubt if that's got anything to do with this business.'

As mentioned in my introduction, the mining community is represented by a least one recorded paranormal experience down a County Durham pit. A correspondent, who signed himself T. Gibbon, described how he had descended Littleburn Colliery to a worked-out seam on a New Year's Eve. He was there to attend to pumps and as he sat down to catch his breath, in the light of his lamp, he spotted something ominous. It was a death's head hawkmoth. Unable to swat it with his cloth cap, his attention was caught by the sound of a pit pony's hooves and harness and chains approaching. As the din ceased, an arm lunged from out of a manhole and made a grab for the phantom pony. As instantly as both had appeared, they vanished. Upon inquiry, the terrified observer discovered that a year or so previously a young pit lad had been trampled to death by a runaway pony.

SIX

REVENANTS, OMENS AND SADNESS

WHEN I have unpleasant dreams they usually hark back to when I was employed as a sub-editor at the *Hartlepool Mail*. Invariably, they involve anxiety over meeting a deadline. Either that or there is some form of threat. On the night I'm about to describe from more than a decade ago, I was having a nightmare in which I confronted a group of teenage shoplifters who turned nasty and attacked me. I awoke suddenly and sat bolt upright. Ahead of me in the darkness was an even darker shape. It was the figure of a human; the body was tall and wide of girth, which made the head look comparatively small. There were no features whatsoever or even semblance of clothing outlines. As the shape moved away towards the door I had the impression it was a stocky man with his back to me – whatever it was then vanished.

This was in the middle of the night and as I sat there I knew it had not been a burglar, despite awakening from a nightmare feeling fearful. I was able to move, so it was not the 'hag experience' investigated by David Hufford in his book *The Terror That Comes in the Night*, in which he compares present-day bedroom invaders with folkloric accounts of licentious succubi and incubi, and then associates both with the medical hypothesis of sleep paralysis. Nor was it hypnagogic or hypnopompic, those hallucinations which people have usually when they have not fully fallen asleep nor were fully awake, which I then believed were the only times it happens. Now I know differently – at least for me. Since the experience I'm describing, I went through a scary month-long period whereby I was waking regularly and seeing human forms in wall decorations, curtains, bookcases and basically anything else in the room. Not only that but clearly defined faces, too, usually mocking, reaching a peak where half a dozen figures were sat around as if at tables in a pub, drinks in front of them but all just staring at me. Thus I concluded that on this occasion what I witnessed was not a hallucination. As I again disregarded the after-image from a dream explanation, I wondered if it was associated with a couple of sculpted heads I had collected during my investigation into the notorious Hexham Heads mystery. I discarded that notion also, as I did not feel the fear I might have expected should my nocturnal visitor have been a fearsome werewolf, so at home in horror movies, or more approachable wulver, of folklore fame. I felt I knew the answer the moment I discerned the shape – it was a local character 'Big Jimmy' Harrison, and that he had died.

Jimmy Harrison had been a shot-blaster and former sea-coal gatherer who had contracted Legionnaire's disease, rumoured – wrongly as it turns out – to have not taken adequate precautions to protect himself because a face mask impeded his breathing caused by an asthmatic condition. I knew he was on a life-support machine at the University Hospital of Hartlepool, where he had lain in a coma for a month. As I laid in bed coming to terms with the encounter, as I presumed it had been, I wondered whether he had passed away and then if his possible appearance fitted the lore of revenants visiting relations and friends for a last time and if so, why me, and rather bizarrely, how did his shade know where to find me? Weird train of thought, for we were not friends by any stretch of the imagination, merely pub-going acquaintances.

Over the years he had been a familiar figure in the bars of Hartlepool and Seaton Carew, whose beach he had raked for coal washed up by strong tides. Whenever our paths crossed he would give a friendly nod and a 'Hi'. When I read a letter in the *Hartlepool Mail*, signed 'J. Harrison' in defence of sea-coal gatherers, who – in my opinion – were being persecuted unfairly by the local council, I went over to him in the Marine Hotel and commended him on such an articulate and well-argued defence. He gave me a wry smile before admitting he was not the 'J. Harrison' in question, that was his brother John. I asked him to pass on my compliments for so cogent a plea in support of people trying to earn an honest crust in a hard job in all weathers at whatever time the tides dictated. We chatted about the debate and I said that the *Mail* had to be impartial and that was why I wrote the non-committal headline 'Burning issue' for a full-page synthesis of the pros and cons. The visitation was on a night early in August 2001. That lunchtime I went down for a midday drink in the Marine and as I entered the bar a bricklayer acquaintance, Mattie McLoughlin, was sat on a stool. He put a hand on my shoulder and I knew straightaway what was coming. 'I've got bad news, Paul,' he said with a sad nod. 'It's Jimmy,' I blurted. 'What time?' For my sins, I hoped he would say it was the middle of the night, but Big Jimmy had passed away around noon to 1 p.m. the previous day. I was tempted to share my night-time experience, but shied away, thinking it would sound too strange.

Struck down in the prime of life at 44 years, Jimmy left a wife and grown-up son living in Jutland Road. His place of employment, Universal Protective Coatings, was ruled out as a possible source of infection.

But was what I seemed to witness a post-mortem apparition? Parapsychologists have their own criteria for such ghostly happenings, such as that a person should have been dead for at least twelve hours and sometimes the phantom seems to have a sense of purpose and on occasions attempts to communicate a message to the witness.

Typically brief, such encounters probably depend upon a reaction to all manner of circumstances, from panic to elation, indifference to puzzlement to incredulity, or as in my case curiosity and bemused acceptance. Additionally, few genuine ghost tales have a beginning, middle and end. This personal experience of mine has just such a rare narrative structure – of sorts.

From involuntary contact with the spirit world, here next is a case of deliberately seeking involvement. For three years Tom and Anne Lowther, of Wood View, Trimdon Station, were troubled by minor disturbances of the type attributed to traditional poltergeist behaviour: doors opening and shutting without a human presence, footsteps, the sound of clawing across a ceiling and a cooker turning itself on and off. In order to discover why their house was plagued by mysterious happenings they attributed to supernatural intervention, the young couple decided to see if a Ouija board could make sense of their troubles. During the session the words 'Lie Ned' were spelled out and the next day they learned that Tom's uncle, Ned Lowther, who lived in Wheatley Hill, had died. 'It gave us both a terrible shock,' said Tom.

Personal experience of trying this form of contact has left me in no doubts that results can be expected, but the content can be wholly unexpected and disturbing. With a now long-forgotten purpose in mind, instead of what we hoped for my wife and I seemed to contact a neighbour who was a former colleague of mine and we stopped the experiment, never to attempt a repeat session. On the one previous occasion we held a similar séance we were being led by a spiritualist

friend called Peggy Armstrong, then living on Hartlepool's Owton Manor estate. With short black curly hair and an English rose complexion, suddenly before mine and my wife's eyes Peggy's face became transformed. Her features became distinctly Oriental – those of an elderly Chinese man. Again proceedings were abruptly halted.

Contact with the spirit world can be a tricky business and an exercise which can cause deep suspicions, if not downright hostility in some quarters. Tabloid tales of possession abound and the movie industry has milked this negative side to the full with films such as *Ouija*, *Ouija Board*, *Witchboard* and *The Exorcist*. For others, contact equates with comfort and a connection with departed loved ones. A medium or the Ouija board forms most people's first contact with the 'occult' and there are few alive (or dead for that matter) who have not heard of the 'talking-board' as it was first termed. The Ouija board properly appeared in the United States in 1890 and has been both popular and denounced from pulpits as the Devil's work ever since. But how do users gain free unlimited calls to the 'other side' and with no annual service contract?

Omens of death were introduced into the paranormal mix by the couple at the centre of unsettling events in their East Durham home of twenty-five years in Maritime Crescent, Horden. Retired joiner Tom Waller, aged 61, and his wife Caroline, 57, who were both disabled, claimed spooky happenings had begun twelve years previously in 1964 when she saw the figure of a middle-aged woman disappearing into a bedroom, but when she followed it there was no one there. Other members of the family saw the wraith on various occasions before everything returned to normal. In the mid-1970s there was a resumption of paranormal activity, with a catalogue of classic indicators of ghostly goings-on: rooms suddenly becoming icy cold, sounds of footsteps but no one visible and the air supply cut off to a fish tank.

But what of the 'omens of death'? Five days before 6-month-old granddaughter Lorraine died suddenly in her cot at her home in Victoria Street, Shotton, the Wallers's 11-year-old granddaughter Karen was staying with them. After she turned off the bedroom light there was the sound of glass crashing all around her. Mrs Waller recalled:

Karen told me she dived under the bed-clothes absolutely terrified, but after a few minutes she found the courage to put the light back on. Nothing had been disturbed. She put the light out again and the smashing of glass started once more. Then she heard footsteps walking out of the room and on to the landing, and the noise stopped. I was convinced that it was a warning that someone close to us was going to die.

Five days later Lorraine was found dead. Then a week later, Mrs Waller was awakened by a loud thump which she wrongly presumed was her husband falling out of bed. He was fast asleep but four days later her 67-year-old uncle, Jack Gray, died of

Currently a visitor centre in Easington Village, Seaton Holme is a thirteenth-century former residence of an archdeacon who became England's only pope. It is also unique among the 'Land of Grey Ladies' for having a lone White Lady ghost. No wonder the building is Grade I listed. (© Paul Screeton)

a heart attack at his home in neighbouring Newcastle Avenue. From then on there was a fear that any loud sound presaged another tragedy in the family.

A series of articles in the *Hartlepool Mail* by the local historian Robert Wood led a Miss Reilly to enquire if he knew anything of Elwick Hall's resident ghost. Their joint information has allowed me to piece together a romantically sad tale. In its original form, a visitor going up the main stairs of this historic country house with a Grade II listed building status, would be faced by the dressing room door. It was this room which was supposed to be haunted. It was also said the ghost appeared on 29 June, St Peter's Day, which happens to be Elwick's patronal festival. Miss Reilly's aunt, who was 89 at the time of the original article, actually saw the ghost. It was around the year 1900 and she was in the dressing room when she saw a little girl sitting on the window seat in the moonlight. She asked her what she was doing there but the child did not answer. She asked her who she was and again there was no reply. Then the girl simply disappeared. Miss Reilly's aunt was alarmed and went to the adjoining room, which was occupied by the rector's daughter, Miss Reilly's mother. Upon telling her what she had seen, there was only the comment: 'You had better come and sleep in here if you feel frightened.' The next day she was told that the room was supposed to be haunted. When some alterations were being made, workmen took out the window seat and under it was found the skeleton of a little girl. Why was she not properly buried? Who was she? Is the spectre still there, only to be seen on St Peter's Day?

My last tale in this section takes us close to Durham City and is located where a country girl crossed in love took her own life in a field close by Stob Cross. There is a tragic poem recording the event and gives a taste of the depth of melancholy attached to this gruesome series of events.

> See where the ring-dove haunt yon
>   ruined tower,
> Why ivy twines amidst the ashen spray;
> There still she hovers round the
>   lonely bower,
> Where anguish closed her
>   melancholy day.
> A dove she seems distinguish'd from
>   the rest,
> Three crimson blood drops stain her
>   snowy breast.

Indeed here stood a ruined dovecote haunted by a brood of wood pigeons and around it her spirit dwelt, drawn to the spot where she had enjoyed trysts with a traitorous lover. She took the form of a milk-white dove with three distinct crimson spots on its breast. Her treacherous lover, the deceiver, who could win maiden's heart, ruin, and leave her, drowned himself in the Floatbeck some years after the girl's death and was buried at a crossroads with a stake – or stob – driven through his body; hence the name Stob Cross.

SEVEN

HIGHWAYS, MARITIME AND RAILWAYS

THE granddaddy of road ghost stories is the universal Phantom Hitch-Hiker (PH-H). Actually, that should probably read granddaughter, for these tales almost always involve a female and a young one at that. Also she is generally the most physically substantial within the spectral spectrum. She looks bodily real, opens doors and speaks. She is also one of the most controversial. Folklorists treat this repeating story as following a typical pattern but more developed than other formidably common motifs such as the White/Grey Lady, Black Monk and Black Dog, all of which form part of the essential canon of ghostlore. Forteans are wary but more open-minded about PH-H stories than folklorists, who regard them as purely contemporary legends, migratory ones at that, with no true basis whatsoever. Fellow fortean folklorist – if that is not quite an oxymoron – Michael Goss has studied this matter in depth over many years and his excellent book *The Evidence for Phantom Hitch-Hikers* finds some substance in a few individual cases. It is as if on occasion a sleepover scare story escapes fiction and crosses over into the twilight world of quasi-reality. And why not? Surely at the core of ghostlore is the fact that it is not all in the mind, fevered imaginations, mis-perceptions and all manner of denigrations the sceptical can throw at it.

Which brings us to Crimdon Dene: one of several narrow coastal scenic valleys gouged into the magnesian limestone of East Durham by meltwater as the Ice Age ended and glaciers retreated. But this story is rather more modern and comes from 1962. One spring evening a young man was riding his motorcycle from Hartlepool to Horden. When he reached Crimdon Dene he saw in the glare of his headlamp a girl in a white mackintosh standing in the middle of the road. She was obvi-ously not going to move out of his way so he pulled up and asked if anything was amiss or did she require a lift. She asked if he was going through Blackhall and if so, could he take her home. He agreed and she got on behind him and he obliged by delivering her at the street she indicated. She dismounted and without a word entered one of the houses. He was a little taken aback that she did not proffer her thanks, but on relating the experience to his friends the next day there was a sudden silence. He asked what the matter was and was asked to describe where he picked her up, what she was wearing and her address. He answered the questions and his pals informed him that the girl he had described had been killed at that exact spot where he picked her up; that she was wearing an identical mac and that the street to which he had taken her was where she had lived.

Another version of this popular legend appeared in the *Sunderland Echo*. Jimmy Taylor of Coxhoe recalled that after a transfer to Blackhall colliery in 1968, he and his fellow pitmen were taking a break and eating their packed lunches when the conversation came around to a fitter who left the mine one morning

at 4 a.m. to travel home to Peterlee on his motorcycle. As he rode along the road towards Horden he spotted a young woman. She was standing in the middle of the road, dressed in a long party frock. When the biker pulled up, she asked if he could give her a lift home. When they arrived at the address she had given, the miner looked back but no one as there. Fearing she had fallen from the motorbike, he retraced his journey, but there was no sign of the partygoer. Baffled, he travelled home and went to bed. The next day, curiosity got the better of him and he called at the girl's address on his way to his shift. When a woman answered he asked if her daughter had arrived home safely from her party the previous night. He explained that he had given her a lift at 4 a.m. but that she has disappeared. With a look of

Not only is the road crossing Crimdon Dene the scene of an archetypal phantom hitch-hiker tale, but is also where motorist Geoff Denton and his wife Myra spotted the Hartlepool Puma cross in front of their car and vanish into this beauty spot. (© Paul Screeton)

shock on her face, the woman explained that her daughter had been killed on that same stretch of road a number of years previously after celebrating at a party. The miner explained further that she had spoken to him and given that address. The woman agreed that it must have been the spirit of her daughter and that, however extraordinary, she believed what the young man had told her. Mr Taylor concluded his letter by asking hypothetically, 'Could this have happened I wonder. Is this story true?'

Well, yes and no. Not in strictly physical terms, but if we are willing to accept there can be instances – however transient – of separate realities, then it could be feasible. An archetype can, when sufficiently strong enough, replicate itself to conform to the fashions of the times and codes of behaviour. Of all traditional ghost stories this is probably the most powerful, complete, universal and repetitious of them all.

A little out of our geographical area, but another regional example and true to the motif, is the similar case of yet another girl hitching a lift in Springwell Road, Sunderland, who wished to be taken to Thorney Close. On the way, the biker almost lost control on a bend and when he checked the safety of his pillion passenger she was nowhere to be seen. He frantically retraced the route by which he had come but to no avail. Remembering the address she had given, he called there only to learn from the woman who answered the door that her daughter had died a year previously to the day – in a motorcycle accident. The added detail of the anniversary often occurs in this tale and other ghost stories, though I have always pondered whether Leap Year anniversaries only occur every four years.

In PH-H tales it is the exception rather than the rule to have actual identities of participants and ones who are willing to talk openly about their chilling experience. This does give more credence that there may be some substance to the occurrence in certain circumstances; that not all are simply bar-room 'foaf' (friend-of-a-friend) stories. A case in point involves a girl who, in August 1979, flagged down the last United bus from Peterlee to Durham City at Pittington End, near Haswell Plough. She requested to be taken to Sherburn Hill, but admitted to having no money for her fare. Driver Don Weatherall took pity on her, thinking she might have been put out of a car and agreed to take the damsel in distress to her destination. But when he arrived there she had simply vanished. He checked to see that she had not fallen asleep or even collapsed, but his thorough search of the bus was all in vain.

'It was impossible for her to have got out while the bus was moving. I searched high and low for her. I was terrified. I was only too pleased to pick up some passengers on the way to Durham,' Mr Weatherall admitted. When he told his workmates about his late-night encounter, further variants of the ghost tale came to light, thus going some way to substantiating his experience. She had accepted a lift from a motorcyclist, but when he stopped he found he found the pillion seat to be empty. In another she was hitch-hiking and the motorist who picked her up later found no trace of her. Apart from the dubious assumption that the three modes of transport all involved the same ghostly girl, other aspects of interest are that Mr Weatherall learned a girl had been killed in a road accident in the same area some years previously and that she was wearing 'old-fashioned' clothes. Rather than dramatise his story, the journalist handling the original report contacted the police for a comment, but a spokesman was quoted as telling him that they knew of no such accident as described nor any reports of a ghost seen on that particular stretch of road.

The theme is pure folklore, yet as I have demonstrated, particularly in the latter case, even the hardened folklorist must admit to an unease that some case histories sound disturbingly authentic: known as examples of ostension, whereby fiction crosses over into fact, or at least faction. Here is where forteans have the upper hand as there are more than a single place haunting for in some instances the spirit – or whatever it is – has a discourse with the driver before vanishing. With such ambiguity afoot, no wonder science throws up its hands in despair and retreats to the laboratory.

However, recently a rather far-fetched theory has been floated by psychologists to explain PH-H phenomena. 'Inattentional amnesia' argues that driving along dark, lonely roads creates a mental state where events happen but are only dimply recalled. Drivers are aware of arriving at a destination with no memory of the last few miles, as if they drove on 'auto-pilot'. This implies the drivers could pick up a passenger but forget dropping them off and believe they had vanished or fallen off in the case of a motorcycle. Paucity of named witnesses does not help the supernatural aspect, nor does the faction within the contemporary legend milieu who bar any paranormal motif. For psychologists to be so dismissive of the PH-H

is unscientific hubris, but I am sure a dialogue between non-dogmatic psychologists and open-minded folklorists could be fruitful. Where better to start than the pros and cons of inattentional amnesia (or highway hypnosis')?

In addition to Mick Goss's investigative *The Evidence for Phantom Hitch-Hikers*, the doyen of contemporary legend scholars, Prof. Jan Harold Brunvand of the University of Utah, began his distinguished writing career with a book entitled *The Vanishing Hitchhiker: American Urban Legends and Their Meanings*. Brunvand described this as 'the classic automobile legend'. She (the hitchhiker) may not spend a lot of time travelling and never completes the journey, but that is compensated for by the key aspects having a long and illustrious pedigree. American versions collected from 1876, 1912 and 1920 place the PH-H in a horse-drawn vehicle even. As for her later preference for more modern forms of transport, this amounts to what is generally known as cultural tracking – or keeping up with the times. As technology becomes more sophisticated, so the legend adapts itself. It is a shame that the East Durham hitchers are so mundane, when elsewhere more exotic quasi-physical travellers are more talkative and deliver prophetic messages. Before leaving the topic, forgive me for making an observation which shows how far behind and out of step with popular culture folklorists can be. Jan points in an updated footnote to a later edition that when he first published the book in 1981 the vanishing hitch-hiker was the only urban legend with a specific motif number assigned to it in the standard folkloristic reference works – E332.3.3.1. Were the folklorists simply away with the fairies?

Management at Hartlepool brewers Camerons obviously chose the name The Saxon for its compact estate pub during the mid-1960s for a specific reason. However, as the years passed no one was sure whether it was because of its being built on land supposed to have originally been a Saxon burial ground or in honour of a ghost. A motorist had reported that as he drove down the stretch of coast road from Sunderland to Hartlepool (the A1086), which passes where the pub was later built, he saw in the headlights the spectral figure of a Saxon warrior strolling at right angles. Sadly, the mists of time have also erased any further details of this highway encounter. So, whether The Saxon was named as such because of the purported ancient cemetery or after the jaywalking

immigrant plunderer, it is good to have an aspect of the region's history recognised.

Modes of travel is the theme of this chapter, but as for being on horseback, equestrian spirits are thin on the ground and the best I can muster is a phantom horseman who appears around midnight near Blackhall Rocks' Mortuary Bank. One elderly resident related how he saw a figure wearing clothing of an earlier period dismount at the bank top and look out to sea before he and his mount disappeared. Sadly there are no further details.

In contrast, seafarers are notorious as a profession for telling yarns and being superstitious, so I doubt the then vicar of St Oswald's and an honorary Missions to Seamen chaplain, the Reverend Anthony

Only half a mile from Crimdon Dene is a spot on the A689 where a driver saw the figure of a Saxon warrior crossing in front of him, hence the new pub being named The Saxon. The sighting supports the argument for a warrior leader named Arthur being present in the area to repel such invaders. (© Paul Screeton)

Hodgson, was hardly surprised when approached for assistance by sailors on a coaster docked at Hartlepool while navigating between Hull and Amsterdam. The seamen aboard the *Somersbydyke*, in Central Dock, believed they had a spectral stowaway on board and had called for spiritual intercession. 'They said they had seen phenomena on board the ship that they could not explain,' the minister told the *Hartlepool Mail*:

> The men were normal intelligent sailors and when I got down to the ship they were obviously frightened of something, so I took their request seriously. I have no opinion on what they claimed to experience, but I endeavoured to ease their minds by saying prayers in various cabins on the ship. I was surprised when I got the request to come to the ship, but I think priests have to deal with the unusual quite often. In this case I went along to discuss the sailors' problem and to help them with prayers. In this case I was trying to drive out the men's fears about the ship.

Sadly the newspaper report lacked much colour, which is more than can be said for Tony Hodgson, one of those maverick 'turbulent priests' who bedevil their bishops. He subsequently got in touch with his opposite number at the Missions to Seamen refuge in the Netherlands port where it next docked to check whether his ministry had been effective and learned the crew were pacified. Nothing more was heard of the *Somersbydyke*'s haunting and the cargo vessel went on to sail the Seven Seas in a further six guises before being cut up in Calcutta in 1998.

Unlike the crew of *Somersbydyke*, a mariner who was not perturbed by ghostly goings-on aboard his vessel was skipper Steve Ding, then living in Furness Street, Hartlepool. The chief officer on ships exporting Nissan cars, he had bought a 40-year-old trawler and was renovating it to become a floating restaurant and bar for when he immigrated to Portugal. In addition to the creaking noises expected from an aged 350-ton vessel, Steve and other workmen regularly heard someone walking about on the decks above, while footsteps could also be heard approaching and retreating, doors opening and closing, and lights going on and off. When the ship *Scottish King*, whose working career had been spent off the north coast of Scotland, was given a new berth beside Jackson's Landing mall, the psychic energies seemed to have transferred to the shopping emporia. Steve told the *Hartlepool Mail*: 'The staff at Jackson's Landing are now saying they've heard strange noises in the mall. There's been tills ringing and lights going on and off for no reason.' Philosophically, Steve came to accept he owned a 'ghost ship' and regarded his companion as a lucky mascot, even naming it 'McTavish'. 'It's not a nasty, menacing presence at all,' he added. Twelve years later, having been partly converted into a houseboat, the *Scottish King* was towed across Hartlepool Bay to a yard at Haverton Hill. But had McTavish jumped ship for 'life' in the marina or had he chosen a noisy shipyard. Perhaps, we'll never know.

Another ship renovation project whose restorers had come to terms with a resident ghost was nineteenth-century frigate HMS *Trincomalee*, built of teak in 1817 in Bombay and for a period known as Foudroyant. It is the oldest British warship afloat. During a chequered career, one of the crew was 'The Man They Couldn't Hang', Devonian John 'Babbacombe' Lee, named after the location where he was said to have murdered his employer, a crime for which he was convicted, but after three failed attempts to hang him his sentence was commuted to life imprisonment and he was freed in 1907. Little is known of the haunting, but the spirit became known affectionately as 'Chalkie' by the tradesmen working on the renovation. Perhaps a more astute and tourism-inclined stewardship would have bent the facts and named the phantom spirit 'Babbacombe' or at least 'John'.

Actually, the connection between ghosts and ships may have substance according to researcher David Hanson: 'There is a theory about the connection between the water and paranormal activity,' he claims. 'The theory is that the water flowing underneath the hull helps exchange ions or some form of energy that provides more energy for the spirits to manifest or do the things they want to do.' If the theory holds water, Hanson feels that a ship with a good history will be more haunted than the average house.

As for railways, I cannot offer a ghost train but I can produce a haunted locomotive. This tale was not told at a slumber party or around a campfire, but during a game of dominoes. Brian Nielsen had introduced railway-fitter Hugh Watson to the 'doms school' at Seaton Carew Sports and Social Club and if he was not working shifts and in the vicinity he would join us for a session. Hughie told me he was hoping

Thornaby Traction Maintenance Depot's 'pet' engine would be preserved when its working life ended. He then added that Class 37 freight locomotive No. 37069, which was named after its home depot as *Thornaby TMD*, had a resident ghost.

For Hugh Watson, author of erudite railway book *The Deltic Years*, every day was a busman's holiday. As a loco maintenance fitter at the depot, when centenary celebrations were held at Darlington's Bank Top station, Hugh was there helping to look after preserved Deltic class loco No. 55009 Royal Highland Fusilier. On the adjacent track was one of his Teesside depot charges, pristine No. 37069, close to its 1962 birthplace at Robert Stephenson and Hawthorns' works in the famous railway town.

Hughie recalled:

One night I was in the Deltic's cab and glanced across at 69 and was convinced someone was in her cab. I knew at the time no one should have been there so I went to investigate. When I reached the loco I looked in both cabs and engine-room windows. There was no one there, but there was a definite feeling that someone was around. After a while I returned to Royal Highland Fusilier and occasionally looked across at 69. Suddenly a diesel horn sounded. It was definitely not the Deltic, and no other working loco was in the station. It must have been 69 but no person was near her. All I could say, looking at her, [there] was a very strange aura around.

A couple of days later it was an extremely hot summer Saturday afternoon and Bank Top station was very busy.

The ghost in the machine – literally. The spirit of a former driver depot favourite Class 37 No. 37069 Thornaby TMD seems to be still playing pranks on staff. (Alan Hopkins)

Hughie takes up the story:

All of a sudden my son Craig burst into the Deltic shouting 'Dad, *Thornaby TMD*'s on fire!' Immediately a friend and I charged over to 69 and noticed what looked like smoke coming through the engine room louvers. My friend opened the engine-room door and became engulfed by the contents of the fire bottles, causing slight injury to his arms. After making sure he was OK, I returned into the cab alone to make certain nothing was wrong. I was alone, yet I knew I wasn't, although there was no one there. Yet the hairs on the back of my neck stood up and there was a definite presence. I turned and went into the engine-room. No one was there. I ran through into the other cab. No one was there either: it was very eerie. Once recomposed and realising that previously that day the loco's cabs had been open to the public, I checked to see if the fire bottle levers had been pulled, but they hadn't. Nor had there been a fire in the engine room. It appeared the fire bottles had gone off on their own accord. I looked around and thought, 'This isn't real'. But it was.

When the celebrations ended, 37069 was scheduled to haul the Deltic and a supporting Peak class loco back to Thornaby depot. Initially 37069 refused to start, but after attention it burst into life and accomplished its allotted task. When Hughie recalled the bizarre happenings to colleagues at the depot, a strange picture began to emerge. It was said at Thornaby depot that night or day, if a horn should sound or fire bottles went off without explanation or no one present, 'It's only 69 at it again'. Very typical of poltergeist behaviour – but a curious choice of location. But was there a possible explanation? Yes. The loco had earlier been numbered D6769 and while hauling a southbound freight between Northallerton and York, an approaching Deltic locomotive on an express threw up an object which smashed through the windscreen, hitting the driver on the head and killing him, but luckily not disabling the second man. Hughie said:

Persons approaching the loco are said to have seen the apparition of a man sat in the driver's seat, believed to be the fatefully-killed driver. One driver explained he never felt alone on 69, and many times had occasion to look in the engine-room or back along the loco to see if anyone was there – but there never was. Once I learned of 69's reputation, I could hardly believe it.

To bring the story up to date, after privatisation 'The Ghost', as 37069 was also known at Thornaby depot, was in 2001 slated for component recovery and scrapping by its new owners, English, Welsh and Scottish Railway. Hughie always hankered after having the loco preserved at the end of its useful life and indeed such an effort was made in 2001. The preservation bid failed at the time as it was bought by Direct Rail Services, for use hauling flask trains between power stations such as Hartlepool and the Sellafield reprocessing plant, in Cumbria. Old 69 lingers on stored in the DRS reserve pool of locos and may yet meet the scrap man – or happy retirement on a preserved line, where she can spook volunteers and visitors.

EIGHT

SHAMANIC LANDSCAPES, HAUNTED SKIES

THIS story involves no ghost as such, but then a poltergeist is invisible. This is a tale of true terror, but there was nothing to see. This is a tale of sheer, utter panic. Also, I can vouch for its veracity, for I was that witness.

Without exaggeration, I had never felt so frightened in my life. There was nothing to see that was scary and absolutely no visible danger. Yet there I was in a country lane, in broad daylight on a bright summer's day, feeling utterly terrified. There was menace in the air. There was a malevolence – but what? It was as if an unseen portal to another realm had opened up, and was all the more terrifying for that invisibility.

I had paused while cycling, having been out early to take photographs. My circular return home took me along a rough path known to everyone locally as Blackberry Lane. The name itself sounds harmless, but remember bramble bushes have thorns. It was in Seaton Carew, a public pathway between allotments and a railway coast line. Yet it was as if I had entered a Lovecraft horror story. At the northern end was Station Lane and opposite was the Station Hotel at the time; in the other direction an industrial estate. I had paused where the road to the station forks on the left. All of a sudden I was gripped by a dread greater than anything I could have imagined possible. It was a stifling, gut-wrenching fear: I actually felt as if my life was in imminent peril. It was so overwhelming I thought it was going to overpower me. Fight or flee? There was no option when the enemy was so powerful in strength and indiscernible. In fact, I neither debated nor hesitated. I pedalled away furiously as fast as I could; cycling straight across the main road, oblivious to the likely presence of oncoming traffic. I fled and I'm not ashamed to admit it. For I had disturbed a shapeless, nameless evil phantasmagoria such as would have made Hell itself tremble and shake with horror.

Only later did I realise that my awesomely daunting experience occurred directly opposite the doorway of the Station Hotel, with its pair of protective guardian wood carvings. Surely these had been crafted deliberately to ward off such an untimely daylight witching hour intrusion as I had inadvertently stumbled upon? Nevertheless, surely a site cannot be inherently evil; there must be an entity to cause panic?

A document claims the pub was built in 1871 at the behest of Michael Bell, a former stationmaster at Seaton Carew railway station, but when Dave Borland was landlord he told me he had been in the attic and found documents relating to the inn dating from 1850. From the evidence of adjoining stables still standing and used as a bottle store in latter years, I had sussed it was a coaching inn, possibly predating the coming of the railway. Above the doorway, and probably dating from original construction, was a porch with two facial figures either side of the entrance. These must surely be guardians, or in folklore nomenclature, apotropaic figures. They must have been put there by someone in the know to ward off whatever might occasionally manifest opposite. Their sole purpose was to deter some lurking demon from taking shape and terrorising drinkers enjoying the peaceful hospitality of the inn. Or was it a warning to any visiting pagan deity that a bacchanalian session was off limits? In my opinion, those heads denoted a point of contact between human existence and the supernatural otherworld – a territory

Seaton Carew's Station Hotel shortly before demolition. (Alan Hopkins).

Painted white, the guardian heads, which many patrons – and even landlords – failed to notice. (© Paul Screeton)

where spirits and deities dwell, going about their business in a realm to which we mortals are only occasionally privy. It is a shared and invisible domain which is just as real as our everyday landscape, but far more dangerous and wondrous. Dr Anne Ross, the leading Romano-British era scholar, observed that the Celtic goddesses were 'bound and rooted to the land, whereas the gods moved with the seasons and conditions', and this applied to such specific locales as the one I had encountered.

The recent revival of interest in Wicca, occultism, mediumship and the supernatural is evidence that beneath the veneer of Christianity and enlightenment thought overthrowing blind superstition and ancient customs, there lies a bedrock of centuries of paganism, the old gods and goddesses and ancestor worship.

In those olden days it was the habit of witches – being shunned by the rest of society and so being naturally solitary souls – to have as a companion a cat or other animal. Often these were no ordinary moggies, but felids imbued with special powers. Not ghosts as such, of course, but having a strongly supernatural element so as to place them in a wholly otherworldly dimension. Here are a couple of Nort East variants to demonstrate this sinister relationship between the humans dabbling in the occult and their feline accessories to the crime. A truly 'familiar' theme.

A farmer called John Bonner, of Beggar-Bush, between Easington and Castle Eden, was driving past the dene when an animal darted out of a hedge-row and landed behind him on the cart. 'Johnny Bonner, Johnny! When thou gets hyem, tell your cat Catherine Curley's deed,' it instructed in the local dialect. This utterance from a large cat naturally scared the man and after it leapt from the cart he drove off as fast as possible. Upon arriving home, his wife asked why her ashen-faced spouse was so distressed. When finally he spoke, he gasped out the tale of his uncanny encounter. At the point where he repeated the talking cat's utterance, their own cat jumped up, exclaiming in local parlance, 'Aw mun awa,' and dashed out of the house never to be seen again.

Here's a variant on the above, either what's known as a migratory legend or more likely simply a plagiarised early urban/rural myth. This tale of another supernatural talking cat has a Staindrop farmer as central character who one night was crossing a bridge near his home when a cat jumped out, stood and instructed him, 'Johnny Reed, Johnny Reed! Tell Madam Momfoot that Mally Dixon's deed!'

He too reported his scary experience when he arrived home and upon repeating the verse, his own black cat jumped up and exclaimed, 'Is she?' It too ran out of the door and disappeared forever.

Although the notion of talking cats may be ridiculous to educated twenty-first-century minds, in times past many highly placed people took seriously what we today would mock. For instance the Chancellor of the Bishop's Court in Durham chose to believe that a Hart woman, Allyson Lawe, was a notorious enchantress and sorceress. As punishment, he ordered that she appear before the populace in Durham Market Place, in Norton and also pay penance in Hart's beautiful little church. Janet Bainbridge and Janet Allenson were also accused of going to her for advice and potions to cure diseases. Innocuous though this seems, there were those who mistrusted such practices. Hence witches were persecuted. Allyson died in 1588, the year of the Spanish Armada. There was also the scarily named Helen de Inferno.

Nearby Elwick, too, had a wise woman at the turn of the seventeenth century to whom folk from the surrounding district would come for consultations. She must have been quite a character for she went by the awesome name of Old Mother Midnight. The only person to have recorded in print that one of these witches returned to spook her old haunts is Old Mother Midnight. A sub-editor at the *Hartlepool Mail* (then *Northern Daily Mail*) when I began my journalistic career was Fred Allison. Writing in 1947, his purple prose described how, 'For nights when the wind howls round the chimneys and flickering flames lick festive logs there is the weird story of Old Mother Midnight, whose ghostly figure flits among the village trees when the owls are silent and the night is moonless.' Old Mother Midnight was a witch who was burnt at the stake and, because 'they wouldn't have her in the churchyard', her remains were buried as close as possible – just outside the gateway at Hart, where a stone, now indecipherable and built into the wall, recorded the fact.

I have never been able to locate this memorial, never mind trying to decipher it. As with all folklore, this tale is somewhat confused, as written testimony from the time of the witch persecution points to a rather less prosaic explanation for this continuing folk belief, which is still passed on from generation to generation of Hart villagers and sightseers alike. A more substantive account names Ellen Thompson as having been excommunicated by the Church and who was buried outside holy ground by a stile at the north-east corner of the churchyard, where worshippers from that direction would walk over her body and thus ensure her evil spirit would forever lie beneath the ground.

It may come as a surprise to some readers, but there was sexual equality in this department centuries ago and witches had their male counterparts, not as traditional wizards, but 'wise men' or 'cunning men'. One such individual lived in Hartlepool and went by the name of Black Willie. He assured a couple who had consulted him over the loss of two horses during the past year that they had been bewitched by their neighbour in Greatham, a farmer's wife. She in turn sought guidance from the Church in the form of the Reverend H.B. Tristram. This was November 1861, and upon the dubious advice of the wise man, the accusers adopted an appalling method to ascertain the identity of the culprit. After procuring a pigeon and tying its wings, they closed every aperture in the house – even blocking keyholes – and each member of the household stuck pins into it to pierce its heart. They then roasted the bird while keeping a close watch at the window, for whosoever passed was to be revealed as the guilty party. Not surprisingly the woman who lived opposite was the first person to be spotted and the family assumed she was therefore the witch. However, the vicar revealed by his comment, 'though she was

a comely matron, not yet 50 years of age', that had she been 80 and wizened she might have aroused his own suspicions.

As for roasting with regard to witchcraft, it occurs in a piece of more general Northumbrian lore, for it was far from uncommon in the nineteenth century for mothers in Hartlepool, Sunderland and throughout the towns and villages of County Durham, to think children in poor health to be bewitched. To rectify ailments they would purchase a sheep or bullock's heart from a butcher, stick it full of pins and roast it before a fire. According to tradition, this breaks the charm and the infirm child begins to thrive. Also during the nineteenth century, when a woman appeared before Durham magistrates she gave as her defence for stealing a fowl that her only reason had been to roast it at midnight over a slow fire with pins stuck in and all orifices blocked to the air, so her child would become well. The Bench dismissed the case, considering the delusion under which she had acted was at a gypsy's instigation.

My point in addressing such superstitions is to point out that although we would now rather trust the National Health Service than some folk remedy and ritual, many are still practising unhealthy customs and there are those close to nature who still take magic seriously. Here's a case in point, but as I will show it has a bearing on one of East Durham's best-known supernatural folk tales. My wife and I were staying in Aberdeenshire with a well-known female novelist who was interested like me in prehistoric megaliths. She had escorted us around Tomnaverie and Midmar stone circles, but when we reached Sun Honey she declined to enter its precincts, recalling that on her last visit the recumbent stone – the flat one between the two tallest pillars and sometimes referred to as altar stone – had been covered with ritually laid out dead crows. So magic was still very much afoot. Not only that, but I came across an extraordinarily large hare loping about in the grass. When it reached the exit to the enclosed monument it turned to give me a spine-chilling lengthy stare. Witches supposedly could turn themselves into hares. At the time I felt in little doubt that what I had encountered was no ordinary beast of the field.

So, if ghosts are largely insubstantial phantoms, then what of the ability to remain 'physical', but in another form? I refer not to witches' familiars, but sibyls in the form of animals. Almost to the exclusion of any other fauna, wise women chose for a disguise the form of a hare. The animal is extremely flight of foot and has about it an independent air and undomesticated spirit.

> I shall go into a hare,
> With sorrow and sigh and mickle care;
> And I shall go in the Devil's name,
> Ay, while I come home again.

And so the witch begins a transformation into a hare.

Witches have been supposed to take the guise of crows, cats and other beasts, but the form most preferred is the hare. Particularly in rural areas, close observers of nature feel cautious with regard to hares in the same manner that urban dwellers avoid walking under ladders or making sea voyages on Friday the 13th.

In East Durham, an ill-natured, wrinkled old hag of Easington was suspected of being a witch, for although she did work in the fields, her house was always unoccupied and locked on the occasions when the local hunt met. Also the gentry always encountered a hare which led the hounds away from the fox's scent towards Easington, without any customary doublings and windings. The multiplicity of the occurrence created suspicion and eventually one person was so bold as to suggest that the hare might be a witch. Deciding to test the possibility that the hare really was a witch, the master of foxhounds acquired a black bloodhound suckled at a woman's breast, as advised, and set it upon the track of the hare the next time it appeared. The dog followed the hare closely as it made for Easington and kept right behind until the home of the old hag was reached. As the hare rushed for the small aperture in the door – ostensibly for hens to enter and leave – the hound caught the hare's haunch and tore away a morsel of flesh.

When the huntsmen arrived on the scene they found the door barred, but broke it open. Inside there was no sign of the hare, but there sat the old crone, bathed with sweat, shaking in agony and trembling with fear. Blood was streaming upon the floor from a wound. According to legend, she confessed her supernatural subterfuge and begged forgiveness. Charitably she was left alone thereafter for the letting of blood had almost drained her fabulous power. The original eighteenth-century historian-storyteller William Brockie, was somewhat politely scornful in recording this tale, observing that, 'Never again were the gentlemen of the hunt privileged – if I may use the phrase – to follow their game through a miserable widow woman's bolted cottage door.'

Perilous behaviour but Easington Village's shape-shifting witch would take the form of a sheep and roll on the wall of twelfth-century St Mary's church. (© Paul Screeton)

Nevertheless, a witness told Brockie he and others had seen the 'randy-tongued vile woman' in the shape of a white sheep rolling over and over on the top of the local churchyard wall.

As with twenty-first-century urban legends a parallel yarn comes from not too distant Sedgefield, where a party out coursing hares raised one in a field and it also ran directly for a specific house. At the bottom there, too, was a small aperture meant for allowing entry to hens or a cat. However, before the hare could reach safety, a dog caught it by the leg but was unable to retain its grip. Here again the door was found to be bolted and upon breaking in, the party found the occupant of the cottage, an old woman, sweating, puffing breathlessly and nursing a broken leg. No doubt as she changed back into human form she intoned:

Hare, hare, God send thee care,
I am in a hare's likeness just now,
But I shall be in a woman's likeness
even now.

Some writers have even invoked shapeshifting as a possible explanation for the plethora of sightings of anomalous big cats (ABCs). But occult interpretations are by far overwhelmed by the current majority view that the various leopards, pumas, lions and lynxes adding an exotic mien to our countryside are flesh and blood creatures. These beasts leave droppings, hair and paw prints, scratch trees and occasionally kill or maim livestock. Some smaller species have even added to the nation's roadkill tally and a tame puma was trapped in 1993. Some may indeed be former pets released when they grew too big, old or hostile. Whatever the phenomenon is, farmers, policemen and

An idyllic scene from the past in Castle Eden Dene. The deep valley is associated with King Arthur's endeavours at the fringe of his kingdom; the Durham Puma was also spotted here, and equally controversially it has been linked to the mischief of the Easington Hare. (Copyright unknown)

members of the public are witnessing the beasts and newspapers are reporting them. Having personally witnessed a 6-foot 'black panther' run across the path of the car I was travelling in near Wooler, Northumberland in 1983, I still err on the side of caution as to attribution. Natural or supernatural? Despite its seeming 'realness', the folklorist in me draws a comparison with the earlier 'Black Dog' lore, while the paranormalist leans to Patrick Harpur's 'Daimonic Reality' concept of intermediary states or dimensions of being. Back with shapeshifting, an area on the fringe of the Pennine chain claimed to be home to the Rossendale

Lion, and in 1984 a witch calling herself Margansa, aka Barbara Brandolini, perversely claimed to be responsible for sheep killings in the form of a 'panther'.

For convenience, I have adopted those media sound bite descriptions for geographical distribution such as Durham Puma, whose travels were so graphically mapped by police wildlife liaison officer Eddie Bell during the 1980s. This mystery felid was spotted first at Bowburn, then Thinford, Ferryhill, West Cornforth, Fishburn, Peterlee, Wingate and Castle Eden Dene. In addition to the Durham Puma, Eddie identified a separate Peterlee Cat, which was invariably black, while around Beamish lurked a more lynx-like beast with tufted ears. Eddie lived on a smallholding with a menagerie of animals and was well qualified to challenge many sightings as misperceptions of domestic or feral cats and dogs.

East Durham had around 100 ABC reports in the 1986/7 period. Another outbreak of sightings occurred in 1992–3, including sightings on the Hart by-pass and Hartlepool's Brierton and West View districts. Such multiple ABC observations are punningly called 'cat flaps', whereas concentrations of UFO sightings come in 'waves'.

North-East England has had its fair share of unidentified flying objects, without having any spectacular encounters or identifiable 'hot spots'. Our haunted skies history begins back in 1799, when on 12 November several balls of fire were observed over the neighbourhood of Greatham, described as 'luminous serpents'. This particularly scared Hartlepool fishermen out at sea who felt particularly vulnerable. More recently there was a little-known encounter with the UFO phenomenon which I heard of from neighbours. This was a dramatic multiple-witness incident which involved pupils at Golden Flatts Primary School, stunned to see a circular silvery disc hover over their playground at lunchbreak. This Hartlepool school was built in 1951 and the encounter took place in 1977. A former neighbour of mine, Paul Scott, who has since emigrated, was then 7 years old. He recalled:

It was our dinner break. About four of us were messing about at the back of the annexe when we saw a big shining object. Crossways it was like the length of a big lorry. It was white and shiny with some sort of dome. There was no sound. It was hovering stationary above the long grass. It was visible for a few minutes, it felt good. We were impressed. Then the bell went and we went to tell someone, a dinner lady. When we went back it had gone.

NINE

RESURGENCE OF A HAUNTING HOBBY

A NY local newspaper should have its finger on the pulse of changing trends and a quote in the *Hartlepool Mail* recently – regarding one of this book's subjects – did so with regard to ghosthunting. Speaking in his capacity as manager of the Trincomalee Trust, David McKnight told how the ship was now host to 'seven or eight' vigils annually. 'People tend to come on board at about 9 p.m. and they will stay until around 4 a.m.,' he said. 'The paranormal groups which have been on board reported strange noises and strange feelings.'

Obviously the popularity of TV shows such as *Most Haunted* and *6ixth Sense With Colin Fry* have encouraged this resurgence in the supernatural and the spirit world. Despite some disdain from certain long-time psychic researchers, amateur paranormal interest is a massive twenty-first-century phenomenon in its own right (statistically there are now twelve times the number today interested in ghosts than in the 1990s). Yet veteran researchers regard today's ghosthunting as valueless and another delusional parlour game (usually involving pre-vigil alcoholic beverages) akin to the Victorian Ouija board craze.

Depending on the seriousness of the group, equipment – if any – can vary from old-fashioned camera tape-recorders for discarnate EVP voices (electronic voice phenomena) to EMF (electromagnetic field) meters, ionisation detectors, infra-red photography and even Geiger counters.

Parapsychology regards itself as respectable science, but what of psychic, mediumistic spiritualism? Be it secular or religion-based, it does seem to offer an alternative and equally limited access to the discarnate. But be it secular or spiritual, sincere or charlatanism, mediumistic contact catches the spirit of the age, a zeitgeist or as the author Erik Davis calls it, 'the first popular religion of the information age' and 'a modern quasi-religion of necromantic information exchange'.

I am sure if investigators, of whatever hue or experience are involved, they are broadening their minds if they approach the subject without preconceptions or knowing what (paranormally, at least) they might expect. It's hardly original, but remember an amateur built Noah's Ark and professionals the *Titanic*. As a neutral observer and journalist, I wish all shades of experience and opinion. Healthy scepticism should be balanced by credulity towards possible evidence and one should also welcome innovation and co-operation, rather than sneer and close the mind.

All who read this book must have but one question on their minds: what is the nature of hauntings?

SELECT BIBLIOGRAPHY AND FURTHER READING

Anderson, Maureen, *Tales, Trials & Treasures of Seaton Carew* (Published privately, 1991)

Brunvand, Jan Harold, *The Vanishing Hitchhiker: Urban American Legends and Their Meanings* (Pan Books, London, 1983)

Clarke, *A Natural History of Ghosts: 500 Years of Hunting for Proof* (Penguin, London, 2013)

Cleveland Federation of Women's Institutes, *The Cleveland Village Book* (Countryside Books and C.F.W.I., Newbury & Middlesbrough, 1991)

Davis, Erik, *TechGnosis* (Serpent's Tail, London, 1999)

Devereux, Paul, *Haunted Land: Investigations into Ancient Mysteries and Modern Day Phenomena* (Judy Piatkus, London, 2001)

Gill, Walter, *Hartlepool Trail: Three Walks Within the Borough Boundaries* (Hartlepool Civic Society, Hartlepool, 1975)

———, *Second Hartlepool Trail: Three More Walks Within the Borough Boundaries* (Hartlepool Civic Society, Hartlepool, 1979)

Goss, Michael, *The Evidence for Phantom Hitch-Hikers* (The Aquarian Press, Wellingborough, 1984)

Hapgood, Sarah, *The World's Great Ghost & Poltergeist Stories* (Foulsham, Cippenham, 1994)

Harpur, Merrily, *Mystery Big Cats* (Heart of Albion Press, Wymeswold, 2006)

Harpur, Patrick, *Daimonic Reality: Understanding Otherworld Encounters* (Arkana, London, 1995)

Johnson, Kenneth Rayner (Introduction) and various contributors, *Folklore, Myths and Legends of Britain* (Reader's Digest Association, London, 1977)

Knight, David C., *Poltergeists: Hauntings & the Haunted* (J.M. Dent & Sons, London, 1977)

Liddell, Adrian, *An Illustrated History of Wynyard Estate Through the Passage of Time* (Printability Publishing, Wolviston, 1989)

Michell, John and Rickard, Robert J. M., *Phenomena: A Book of Wonders* (Thames and Hudson, London, 1977)

Monck, Bill, *Castle Eden Dene: An Illustrated Guide* (Peterlee Development Corporation, Peterlee, 1980)

Pevsner, Nikolaus, *The Buildings of England: County Durham* (Penguin Books,

London, 1953)

Playfair, Guy Lyon, *The Haunted Pub Guide* (Javelin Books, Poole, 1987)

Randles, Jenny, *Mind Monsters: Invaders from Inner Space?* (The Aquarian Press, Wellingborough, 1990)

_____, *Strange But True? Casebook* (Judy Piatkus, London, 1995)

Screeton, Paul, *Crossing the Line: Trespassing on Railway Weirdness* (Heart of Albion Press, Wymeswold, 2006)

_____, *Quest for the Hexham Heads* (CFZ Publications, Woolfardisworthy, 2012)

Taylor, David, and Homer, Andrew, *Beer and Spirits: A Guide to Haunted Pubs in the Black Country & Surrounding Area* (Amberley Publishing, Stroud, 2001)

Wright, Reginald, *A History of Castle Eden Lore in Search of King Arthur* (Published privately, Blackhall Rocks, 1985 [Two versions])

_____, *Blackhall Rocks and Blackhall in the Parish of Monk Hesleden* (Published privately, Blackhall Rocks, 1985)

St Joseph's R.C. Primary School Research Club, 'Discover Hartlepool' (www.sjpsh.org.uk/documents/news/newsletters/20pp_booklet.pdf, Hartlepool, 2010)

Local Paranormal Groups

North East Paranormal Investigations

North East Paranormal Investigations is an experienced team which runs public tours in the North East of England. Members have a vast amount of experience from house investigations to some of the most impressive sites owned by the National Trust. Members are serious about the paranormal, but what makes them a great team is the professionalism they have, as well as finding the fun side of being a paranormal investigator and being a great group of friends. Website: www.northeastparanormalinvestigations.co.uk

North East Paranormal Society

The similarly-named North East Paranormal Society investigation group is based on Teesside and members travel all over the UK seeking evidence of the paranormal. Find them on www.facebook.com

Northern Ghost Investigations

New members are invited to ghost hunts, forums, etc. Has a database of haunted sites, plus investigations, spirit communication and articles. Website: www.northern-ghost-investigations.com

Something Paranormal

Organises ghost hunts, ghost walks and haunted suppers. For more details: tel. 0777 343 1683. Website: www.somethingparanormal.co.uk
(There are many more such bodies; some hobbyists and many commercial. The internet is the best place to look for local activity.)

National Paranormal Organistions

At national level there are a trio of UK societies worthy of consideration by the serious researcher. These are: ASSAP, the Association for the Scientific Study of Anomalous Phenomena (www.assap.ac.uk), founded in 1981; the Ghost Club (www.ghostclub.org.uk), founded in 1862; and the SPR (www.spr.ac.uk), founded in 1882.

Lightning Source UK Ltd.
Milton Keynes UK
UKOW04f1257120614

233295UK00001B/1/P